GW00372501

Strange Bodies

Strange Bodies

Gender and Identity in the Novels of Carson McCullers

Sarah Gleeson-White

THE UNIVERSITY OF ALABAMA PRESS

Tuscaloosa and London

Manufactured in the United States of America

Typeface is Goudy and Goudy Sans

∞
The paper on which this book is printed meets the minimum requirements of American National Standard for Information Science–Permanence of Paper for Printed Library Materials, ANSI Z39.48 1984.

Library of Congress Cataloging-in-Publication Data

Gleeson-White, Sarah, 1965–
Strange bodies : gender and identity in the novels of Carson McCullers / Sarah Gleeson-White.
p. cm.
Includes bibliographical references and index.
ISBN 0-8173-1267-6 (cloth : alk. paper)
1. McCullers, Carson, 1917–1967—Criticism and interpretation. 2. Women and literature—Southern States—History—20th century. 3. Psychological fiction, American—History and criticism. 4. Identity (Psychology) in literature. 5. Southern States—In literature. 6. Gender identity in literature. 7. Body, Human, in literature. 8. Grotesque in literature. I. Title.

PS3525.A1772 Z635 2003
813′.52—dc21
2002012921

British Library Cataloguing-in-Publication Data available

Contents

Acknowledgments

In no particular order, I would like to thank Louise Miller especially, as well as Hazel Smith, School of English, University of New South Wales, for not only repeatedly reading the manuscript but also for incisively commenting on it; Patricia Yaeger, as well as Louise Westling and Carol Manning, for their incitement to publish; the Humanities Research Centre at the University of New South Wales in Sydney, which generously funded this project with a Writing-Up Grant; all the staff, particularly Shirley Webster, and postgraduate students in the School of English, University of New South Wales, for their ongoing support; and finally, Peter Cook and our daughter, Florence, for seeing it through with me.

Introduction

Carson McCullers and the Grotesque

Leslie Fiedler has described American literature as "a literature of darkness and the grotesque in a land of light and affirmation" (*Love and Death* 29). More specifically, it is the literature of the so-called Southern Renaissance that has become synonymous with the grotesque, and Carson McCullers's work typifies both. Major critical studies of her work comment on the grotesque and its link with the strange world of the gothic, or its function as a bleak and violent response to the modern world, highlighting the ultimate "cheapness of human life" in the South.[1] In sum, the grotesque, it is agreed, not only has a *symbolic* role in McCullers's novels and short stories, but it also forms a *negative*, unproductive view of the world and human activity. I would argue that McCullers's work has suffered greatly under the pall of these delimiting interpretations of the grotesque; the subversive nature of her project has thus necessarily been overlooked. In response, this study seeks to reevaluate the grotesque in McCullers's major novels—*The Heart Is a Lonely Hunter, Reflections in a Golden Eye, The Member of the Wedding,* and *The Ballad of the Sad Café*—to consider what I suggest is their central focus: errant gender and sexuality.[2] To reinvigorate the grotesque and its function in McCullers's texts, I employ Mikhail Bakhtin's concept of the grotesque, which is at once both affirming and revolutionary. In this way, I seek to move McCullers's texts beyond the gloom and doom with which they have been charged for over fifty years.

Very little has been written on McCullers for nearly a decade, and so the enormous richness of her work in positing new understandings of sexuality and gender has been mostly ignored.[3] McCullers's work is particularly fertile for this sort of investigation, written as it was in the 1940s and 1950s, a time of tension between the changing status of women and the southern ideal of womanhood; between a growing liberalism on the one hand and segregation and repressive sexual mores on the other. Furthermore, McCullers, who was well versed in Freudian theory, explored gender and sexual identity in her own life: she considered herself an "invert" and felt that she was "born a man" (Carr, *Lonely Hunter* 39, 167, 159). It is these tensions of identity that inform not only McCullers's novels but also much contemporary theory in which both compulsive conformity and willful transgression "make" subjectivity. These contemporary accounts posit a form of subjectivity that is neither fixed nor transcendent; rather, it is a subjectivity in process, "becoming," a concept that is fundamental also to the Bakhtinian grotesque.

Reading McCullers through the lens of Bakhtin's subversive and metamorphic form of grotesque representation allows us not only to pinpoint but also to underscore and celebrate those radical—and overlooked—features of her novels: resistance and disobedience, sexual and gender anomaly. In this way, I bring McCullers's critical heritage in line with recent debates on gender and sexuality and show how her work is extremely relevant not only in contributing to these debates but also in highlighting their limits and gaps. Further, I focus insistently on accounts of the body in McCullers's texts as well as in current theories of both gender and sexuality. This means that I explore in great detail the marginal configuration of "freakishness," that is, those stubborn bodily forms and behaviors, such as homosexuality and transvestism, that resist normalizing discourses. While the specifically southern setting of all McCullers's novels only highlights the power of such discourses, transgression of them is thus even more forcefully enacted by the physical grotesques—the freaks, queers, and androgynes that populate her strange worlds.

Like Sherwood Anderson's *Winesburg, Ohio,* McCullers's fiction embraces so-called grotesques: a dwarf and a giant; tomboys, cross-dressers, and homosexuals; deaf-mutes and cripples. It is this collection of outsiders—physical and psychological misfits—that invites the classification of McCullers as a writer of the southern grotesque. But, to repeat, McCullers's freaks have become mere symbols of existential angst. In *Understanding Carson McCullers*, for example, Virginia Spencer Carr argues that "[t]hroughout the author's canon, freakishness is a symbol of a character's sense of alienation, of his being trapped within a single identity without the possibility of a meaningful connection with anyone else" (38).[4] Carr's is typical of those accounts that claim that the grotesque embraces themes of alienation, loneliness, lack of human communication, and the failure of love.[5] Whether they represent "[t]he falling apart of the community . . . signalled by the breakdown of communications between persons, by physical and spiritual isolation, . . . by sexual perversion" (Gossett 159) or "a transcendental idea of spiritual loneliness" (Hassan, "Carson McCullers"312), the grotesques of McCullers's worlds are apparently representative of profound anguish. McCullers herself seems to support such an interpretation when she uses the term "grotesque" to describe her characters: "Spiritual isolation is the basis of most of my themes. . . . Love, and especially love of a person who is incapable of returning or receiving it, is at the heart of my selection of grotesque figures to write about—people whose physical incapacity is a symbol of their spiritual incapacity to love or receive love—their spiritual isolation" ("Flowering Dream" 280). It is at this point that this study branches off from earlier negative, and allegorical, responses to the grotesque world of Carson McCullers. I suggest McCullers's freaks are not exclusively symbolic of the alienating (and sexually indifferent) human condition. Rather, they intimately engage issues of subjectivity in the material realms of gender and sexuality.

Feminist interest in the grotesque in McCullers's texts began to problematize "universal human condition" readings in the 1980s by highlighting sexual difference. However, feminist approaches did not theorize the typology of the grotesque in any detail, resorting to the term "grotesque" as shorthand for the freakish or abnormal. Although Gayatri Spivak's "Three Feminist Readings" was perhaps the first feminist response to McCullers's texts, the work of Louise Westling has had a greater influence on feminist readings of the grotesque in McCullers's writings.[6] Westling considers the grotesque in *The Heart Is a Lonely Hunter*, *The Ballad of the Sad Café*, and *The Member of the Wedding* in terms of the constraints of female identity. That is, the woman who does not conform to cultural demands of ideal womanhood is a frightening, grotesque figure. Miss Amelia Evans, "a nightmare vision of the tomboy grown up, without any concessions to social demands for sexual conformity" (Westling 119), exemplifies Westling's conception of the grotesque. Others followed Westling in exploring how cultural expectations of ideal womanhood labeled "different" forms of female identity grotesque. These readings argue that women's secondary sociopolitical status derives from their representation in and by patriarchy as aberration, as abomination,[7] and perhaps not surprisingly, female self-loathing often inflects such representations.[8]

While feminist commentators on McCullers's writings problematize the category "grotesque" in terms of a fraught female identity, others have sought to reject the terms "grotesque" and "gothic" altogether.[9] Most stridently, Mab Segrest, in "Southern Women Writing," contends that the grotesque is dangerously entangled with both racism and patriarchy in the South: "Both patriarchy and racism depend on creating a category of the Other—or freak, not 'normal like me.' In Southern racism, it is the Black person; in patriarchy, the female" (27). Patricia Yaeger, however, responds to Segrest's cautionary approach to the grotesque by emphasizing that "there may be transforming power, still, in the southern grotesque" ("Edible Labor" 156). The "transforming power" of the grotesque is at the heart of my account of McCullers's freaks. The tensions and difficulties inherent in the grotesque are exactly what enable a liberating reading of McCullers's novels, for tension precludes any possibility of stasis and foreclosure in the politics of identity.

Although I concentrate on McCullers's novels in this study, it is her poem "Father, Upon Thy Image We Are Spanned" from the 1951 *Dual Angel* cycle (*Mortgaged Heart* 298) that most neatly describes the dynamics of her grotesque vision as a whole:

> Why are we split upon our double nature, how are we planned?
> Father, upon what image are we spanned?
> Turning helpless in the garden of right and wrong
> Mocked by the reversibles of good and evil
> Heir of the exile. Lucifer, and brother of Thy universal Son
> Who said *it is finished* when Thy synthesis was just begun.
> We suffer the sorrow of separation and division

With a heart that blazes with Christ's vision:
That though we be deviously natured, dual-planned,
Father, upon Thy image we are spanned.

Humanness is twofold, turning helplessly between "the reversibles of good and evil," and suggests the doubleness and juxtaposition of Bakhtin's grotesque in *Rabelais and His World*. The Rabelaisian body is "two bodies in one: the one giving birth and dying, the other conceived generated and born" (26) and has parallels with McCullers's account of realism where she defines the indebtedness of contemporary southern writing to Russian realism in terms of "a bold and outwardly callous juxtaposition of the tragic with the humorous, the immense with the trivial, the sacred with the bawdy, the whole soul of man with a materialistic detail" ("Russian Realists" 258). The grotesque—as both a literary mode and a model of subjectivity—is one of baroque excess and a violent meeting of incompatible elements. In this way, writes Bakhtin, the grotesque "seeks to grasp in its imagery the very act of becoming and growth, the eternal incomplete unfinished nature of being" (52).

McCullers's poem also portrays binaries—such as good and evil—and the hierarchy implicit in them as reversible and so draws us into the carnivalesque mode of inversion that only serves to underscore the temporary and malleable nature of hierarchies, to mock and parody the status quo. In the novels under consideration here, inversion takes place predominantly in the realm of gender and sexuality. As I mentioned earlier, McCullers in fact described herself as an invert, suggesting the reversibility of masculine and feminine identity, and of sexual desire. The repercussions of reading her novels in terms of inversion are enormous as the hierarchies that structure us are questioned and sometimes overturned.

"Father, Upon Thy Image We Are Spanned" also conjures up the powerful and crucial element of the "unfinished" which, as I will show, defines McCullers's portrait of human activity. The unfinished also recalls the Bakhtinian grotesque that is always in process, always becoming, defying the synthesis McCullers mentions in her poem and which defines the "classic body" (*Rabelais* 28–29).

While McCullers and Bakhtin describe grotesque identity in terms of both juxtaposition and the unfinished, they also importantly imagine it in terms of *bodily* experience, as evidenced by the numerous freakish and wrongly formed characters in the novels, and by Bakhtin's incessant emphasis on corporeal contortion. The grotesque body is an overflowing and excessive body of fertility, in "flagrant contradiction" to the classic body, "a strictly completed, finished product" (*Rabelais* 28, 29). Just as the unruly grotesque body, then, is transgressive of classical proportions, McCullers's physical freaks challenge "normalcy."

That identity is "deviously natured, dual-planned" escapes idealization by McCullers in her poem. Rather, she suggests it is a painful position as we restlessly turn from one pole to the other. So, although Bakhtin's theorization of the grotesque opens up new readings of McCullers's texts, there is a significant point of divergence between the two writers. While Bakhtin insists on the gay abandon and vital laughter and mockery that structure Rabelais's writings, there is nothing of carnival gaiety in McCullers's writings. But, as Bakhtin writes, "grotesque images . . . remain ambivalent and contradictory; they are ugly, monstrous, hideous from the point of view of 'classic' aesthetics, that is, the aesthetics of the . . . completed" (25). Similarly, in McCullers's poem there is another side to the ostensibly bleak vision: hearts "blaze" and it is on "*Thy*" image that we are spanned. Without wanting to diminish the very real pain that underlies much of her writing, it is a more positive, or *productive,* angle of McCullers's grotesque vision, as gently suggested in the poem and overlooked in the critical literature, which I focus on in the following chapters.

In this way, then, Bakhtin's model of the grotesque can help us locate the affirming and productive moments—and there are many—in McCullers's account of what it is to be human, as hinted at in "Father, Upon Thy Image We Are Spanned." Like Bakhtin, who writes that "the grotesque . . . discloses the potentiality of an entirely different world, of another order, another way of life" (*Rabelais* 48), McCullers's grotesque is similarly productive of new worlds, new subjects, albeit strange in the context of the dominant motifs of southern gendered and sexual behavior. So, it is juxtaposition, the conflict of seemingly opposing elements—good and evil in the poem; masculine and feminine, normal and abnormal in the novels—which defines the vigor of McCullers's grotesque. In McCullers's view, "nature is not abnormal, only lifelessness is abnormal.

Anything that pulses and moves and walks around the room, no matter what that thing is doing, is natural and human to a writer" ("Flowering Dream" 282).

In McCullers's worlds, then, both men and women risk the grotesque as "unfinished metamorphosis" (*Rabelais* 24), the result of a dynamics of contradiction. By maintaining the category of the grotesque to read McCullers's four major novels, each of the four chapters will explore its different forms: female adolescence, male homosexuality, cross-dressing, and androgyny. In chapter 1's discussion of McCullers's young tomboys, I investigate and expand on the definition of the Bakhtinian grotesque by analyzing its similarities to and differences from the category of freakishness. I also confront the literary topos of the "sensitive youth," an approach which, in the 1950s in particular, defined McCullers criticism. These studies failed to differentiate between male and female adolescent experience; critics grouped Mick Kelly and Frankie Addams with famous (male) literary adolescents, such as Huckleberry Finn and Holden Caulfield, as exemplars of "the familiar journey of initiation" that ends in "a new wisdom about the limits of human life" (Graver 295).[10] Once commentators ceased reading McCullers's young girls as Everymen, they began to consider the girls as somehow flawed, particularly in their reluctance to submit to an ideal of womanhood.[11]

A first notable exception to this approach to the American novel of adolescence is Elaine Ginsberg's "Female Initiation Theme in American Fiction." Here, Ginsberg tackles female adolescence as a category in need of its own terms of description and experience. In examining both *The Heart Is a Lonely Hunter* and *The Member of the Wedding,* as well as stories by Eudora Welty and Katherine Anne Porter, Ginsberg draws the conclusion that of the female characters, "there is none for whom the acquisition of knowledge and the approach of womanhood is entirely positive" (35). Westling's *Sacred Groves and Ravaged Gardens* also focuses on the painful ambiguity of female identity as figured in the image of the female adolescent and as such, contrasts strongly with earlier readings that claim McCullers's portrayal of Mick is one of "affectionate gaiety" and "charming evocation" (Graver 280). Westling argues that the young girls do not represent the tradition of the lively southern tomboy but, rather, "the conflict between serious ambition and the pressure of conventional femininity." Like Ginsberg, Westling concludes that Mick and Frankie are "ambitious, artistic girls who are disoriented and terrified when they are forced to identify themselves as female at puberty" (114).[12]

From the 1970s onward, then, critical accounts of McCullers's adolescents written by women note and remark on gender difference with a focus on the oppression implicit in southern girlhood. The fiction of female adolescence becomes identified with the "novel of initiation into acceptance of *female* limits" (White 109). In chapter 1, I take into account these more acute feminist approaches to female identity in McCullers's fiction. However, my prime focus is on the *changing* female body as a grotesque body: the female adolescent body as a liminal site of *becoming*, which challenges the very notion of "female limits."[13] Although at the conclusion of *The Heart Is a Lonely Hunter* and *The Member of the Wedding* such promise seems all but extinguished by society's demands for "ideal womanhood," McCullers's texts do succeed in producing experimental subjects.

Chapter 2 explores male homosexuality, in *The Heart Is a Lonely Hunter* and *Reflections in a Golden Eye*, as another form of grotesque subjectivity; homosexuality is a part of the carnivalesque world of the transgression and perversion of the "normal," the classic.[14] In this chapter, I highlight McCullers's enormous struggle as she tries to represent odd desire outside of damaging stereotypes. While I outline the more traditional element of her homosexual portraits and ponder its relationship with the strict artistic censorship of the times, I argue that her portrayals of male homosexuality do undermine common assumptions around homosexual men, to do with such binaries as innocence/corruption, masculine/feminine, and nature/culture. What is most absorbing in McCullers's depiction of homosexuality is her apparent fascination with the power of femininity, suggesting that it is a site of great contestation. McCullers's attempts to represent male homosexuality register the difficulty of accessing new language and images to do so. In this respect, she is raising issues of gender, sexuality, and representation, which still haunt debates surrounding subjectivity today.

Although McCullers was perhaps the first southern novelist to write openly of homosexuality (Evans, *Carson McCullers* 60, with regard to *Reflections in a Golden Eye*), male homosexuality remains virtually untheorized in McCullers critical literature and its effects ignored. Several commentators label Mister Singer, Biff Brannon, and/or Penderton as homosexual or bisexual, but they fail to examine more fully the implications of such labeling beyond the claim that the homosexuals represent once more the alienation of McCullers's worlds,[15] perhaps taking as their lead McCullers's own statement that Penderton's homosexuality is "a symbol, of handicap and impotence" ("Flowering Dream" 282). Fiedler locates McCullers more generally within "[t]he *Harper's Bazaar* Faulknerians" or "the homosexual-gothic novelists," whom he defines according to their "celebrations of homosexual sensibility" in the figure of the adolescent. He argues that McCullers's adolescents, "like the circus freaks, the deaf and the dumb," serve as a symbol not only of innocence but also of *exclusion:* "[T]hey project the invert's exclusion from the family, his sense of heterosexual passion as a threat and an offence; and this awareness is easily translated into the child's bafflement before weddings or honeymoons or copulation itself" (*No! In Thunder* 283–84).[16] I engage with this contention, as well as with other tropes that so often structure representations of homosexuality, such as the soldier and the insane,[17] but go further in considering the constant *interplay between* masculinity and femininity, for example, which lies at the basis of configurations of grotesque homosexuality in McCullers's "almost gay" texts (Austen's phrase [*Playing the Game* 95]).

Readings of gender in McCullers's work are of course not new. However, the analysis of gender in chapter 3, which considers *The Heart Is a Lonely Hunter, The Member of the Wedding,* and *The Ballad of the Sad Café*, diverges from earlier accounts in questioning the very categories "feminine" and "masculine." Thus, although Westling, for example, points to the ambiguity inherent in female identity, I examine just how this ambiguity appears in McCullers's texts in both female *and* male identity. By taking as its starting point the carnivalesque trope of masquerade which, according to Bakhtin, overrides hierarchies to challenge the status quo, chapter 3 characterizes gender identity not as something given but rather as "technology."[18] To test this claim, I explore what I argue are the two techniques at work in the gendering process in McCullers's texts—suspension and foregrounding—which produce gender as a kind of volatile *performance*. To reach this conclusion, I deploy Judith Butler's concept of performance, which disavows any notion of original gendered identity, as well as draw on theories of masquerade initiated by Joan Riviere and followed up by Jacques Lacan, Luce Irigaray, and Mary Ann Doane.

Finally, chapter 4 draws together the emphases of the preceding chapters by reading Bakhtin's notion of the "two bodies in one," which underpins his description of the grotesque body, alongside *The Heart Is a Lonely Hunter* and *The Ballad of the Sad Café*. The most immediate figure this "two bodies in one" concept conjures up is that of androgyny, the subject of several articles on McCullers's fiction. This chapter focuses largely on these commentaries and their construction of androgyny. While earlier critics regarded the androgynes as reprehensible freaks,[19] more recent readings are influenced by the writings of Carl Jung and the (predominantly American) feminism of the 1970s of which Carolyn Heilbrun is particularly representative. These readings depict the androgyne as a sexually neuter and static figure. However, this classical depiction is inadequate as a description of the tensions that structure subjectivity in McCullers's texts. I propose instead Bakhtin's figure of "two bodies in one" as an alternative to these classical accounts. This figure rejects synthesis to maintain difference and is particularly illuminating in relation to McCullers because it allows for the dynamism of her grotesque subjects. It is at this point that this study engages most directly with the anxieties that several feminists, particularly Ruth Ginsburg, express about Bakhtin's conceptualization of the grotesque. The principal problem they discern lies in Bakhtin's alleged appropriation of the feminine in his celebration of carnivalesque subjectivity.

By engaging with contemporary accounts of gender and sexuality, I emphasize and celebrate McCullers's menacing and ultimately transgressive vision, and its emancipatory and empowering potential. At the same time, McCullers's struggle to achieve her vision and her lifelong quarrel with matters of gender and sexuality that still plague us today are at the heart of this account of her grotesque subjects. It is her continuing yet often overlooked relevance that makes a reconsideration of her fiction so urgent.

1

Freakish Adolescents

The Heart Is a Lonely Hunter and *The Member of the Wedding*

Most readers of *The Heart Is a Lonely Hunter* and *The Member of the Wedding* describe McCullers's adolescent girls—Mick Kelly and Frankie Addams, respectively—as either freaks or grotesques, arising from the girls' apparent boyishness. However, although there are elements in common, the categories of freak and grotesque are quite distinct. The clarification of these terms radically alters how we read McCullers's narratives of adolescence.

Up until the 1970s, commentaries on McCullers's "sensitive youths" were sexually indifferent, that is, they made no distinction between the varying experiences of male and female adolescents; the young boys and girls were conflated to underpin the universal experience of initiation into adulthood. Later feminist commentaries contested these readings, focusing on sexual difference in order to highlight the specific constraints of entering womanhood in southern society. However, notwithstanding the insistent social demand for conformity that the novels register, McCullers's adolescent portraits embody a dynamics of possibility and thus challenge any notion of female limits. That is to say, the promise of youth does not die out with the adolescents' entry into adulthood. So, although freakishness well conjures up Mick's and Frankie's feeling of oddness in the face of a changing body and an emerging sexuality, and in the face of the demands of the ideal of the southern belle, it in no way accounts for the moments of promise and potential found in McCullers's representations of possible identities. It is the grotesque, rather, which can illuminate these moments.

The female adolescent is particularly amenable to an exploration of the categories of freak and grotesque since, historically, women have been perceived as freakish, a perception stemming from a biblical tradition that considers women "lesser men." Different cultural practices have tended to represent women's "malformed" bodies as fluid and amorphous. For example, "that the female body can change shape so drastically [for example, in pregnancy] is troublesome in the eyes of the logocentric economy within which to *see* is the primary act of knowledge and *the gaze* the basis of epistemic awareness" (Braidotti, *Nomadic Subjects* 80). It is perhaps no coincidence, then, that Bakhtin bases the grotesque body on the Kerch terra-cotta figurines of laughing pregnant hags. The very word "grotesque" itself, derived from "grotto," evokes images of the "cavernous" female body (Russo 1).[1]

The female adolescent is even more "grotesque" than her adult counterpart: not only is she female, but she is in that liminal state between childhood and adulthood and, in the case of Mick and Frankie, between femininity and masculinity. To exist on the threshold obtains within it grotesque possibilities of becoming. In this way, McCullers's young girls are *revolutionary;* they figure as sites of resistance since it is the adolescent, representing the new generation, the future as hope and possibility, in which society so greatly invests. The female adolescent body, as a grotesque site of becoming, challenges the very notion of discrete (feminine) identity. It is vital, then, to establish the category of the grotesque as an extension of the freak.

FREAKISH ADOLESCENCE

Mick Kelly's and Frankie Addams's socially perceived freakishness arises from their boyishness, at a moment in their lives when they should ideally be entering into womanhood. However, the young girls are freakish not only because of their tomboyishness but also, paradoxically, because of their emerging femininity and sexuality. As a result, the girls identify and are identified with sideshow freaks. What might be the implications of this association of adolescence with freakdom?

In the dynamics of freakishness, the category of "normal" is contingent on the category of the "abnormal." In other words, normality and freakdom, or abnormality, are interdependent. In *The Heart Is a Lonely Hunter* and *The Member of the Wedding*, it is the tension between Mick's and Frankie's tomboyishness and the ideal of the southern belle or lady that most obviously makes manifest this interconnected dichotomy.

Ideal femininity is a particularly powerful image in McCullers's novels since the image of the lady was all-pervasive in the South. Even in the New South, the time in which McCullers was writing and her novels are set, the ideal of the worshipful lady prevailed, although such an ideal became more and more transparent with the changing status of women in the 1940s and 1950s. However, as Westling notes, although the mask of the belle and the lady began to peel away, there was no alternative model of female identity (37).

The southern lady, the imminent destiny of both Mick and Frankie, is well captured in *The Member of the Wedding* in the description of "the club members," whom Frankie watches from the kitchen window, "passing slowly before the arbour. The long gold sun slanted down on them and made their skin look golden also, and they were dressed in clean, fresh dresses" (113–14).[2] It is this image of femininity, a type of arrested subjectivity, to which Frankie must aspire. But because she is a tomboy and so resists conforming to the vision, Frankie is unable to join the neighborhood girls' club (17–18).

It seems that both Mick and Frankie fail to fulfill the requirements of womanhood "membership" due to their male identification, clearly at odds with images of proper femininity. Both girls have boys' nicknames. Ideally, naming should establish "appropriate" gender; to assume a male name confounds and plays with such dynamics of identification. Furthermore, both girls look and behave like males: they have short-cropped hair, dress in shorts and sneakers, and yearn to join the armed forces (*H* 215; *M* 175). The stature of the two tomboys further underscores their defiance of the ideal image of the "good little woman."

In the South, while tomboyishness may have been acceptable in the young girl, at puberty she was expected to begin the metamorphosis into southern womanhood. But, since Frankie and Mick persevere with masculine appearance and behavior, society brands them freaks. This idea of freakdom is reflected in Mick's older and "feminine" sister Etta Kelly's criticism of Mick's persistent masculinity: "'It makes me sick to see you in those silly boy's clothes. Somebody ought to . . . make you behave'" (*H* 41), that is, somebody ought to make Mick become a true woman. In *The Member of the Wedding,* it is Berenice who advises the freakish Frankie to "'change from being so rough and greedy and big. . . . You ought to fix yourself up nice in your dresses'" (98).

There are in fact several moments in both *The Heart Is a Lonely Hunter* and *The Member of the Wedding* when Mick and Frankie do attempt to conform to the cultural ideal of womanhood as articulated by Etta and Berenice and as portrayed in the image of the club members. To do so, the young girls must first "cleanse" themselves of freakishness by rejecting their boyishness. So Berenice counsels Frankie to "'[g]et clean for a change. Scrub your elbows and fix yourself nice. You will do very well'" (M 28). Heeding Berenice in her preparations for her date with the soldier, Frankie plans "'to take two baths tonight. One long soaking bath and a scrub with a brush. I'm going to try to scrape this brown crust off my elbows. Then let out the dirty water and take a second bath'" (M 133). Similarly, before her prom party guests arrive, Mick "went into the bathroom and shucked off her old shorts and shirt and turned on the water. She scrubbed the rough parts of her heels and her knees and especially her elbows. She made the bath take a long time" (*H* 97).

Ironically, when Frankie and Mick do attempt to conform to societal demands, they unwittingly undermine the notion of ideal womanhood. For example, Frankie chooses to wear to her brother's wedding an orange satin evening dress with a silver hair ribbon and silver shoes, prompting Berenice to describe her as a "human Christmas tree in August" (M 107).[3] Consequently, Berenice advises her to swap the gaudy orange satin evening dress for "that fresh pink dress," which will increase her chances of meeting "the cutest little white boy in Winter Hill you ever seen" (M 32). In other words, Frankie must not make a spectacle of herself; that is what "bad" women do.

Mick Kelly also dons femininity. While Frankie risks caricaturing femininity, Mick reveals its impracticability as she dresses for her prom party in "Etta's long blue crêpe de chine evening dress and some white pumps and a rhinestone tiara" (*H* 97). Once the neighborhood children begin to destroy the grownup party atmosphere, Mick becomes aware of the constraints of feminine attire. Wanting to jump into a roadside ditch, she realizes that with "her tennis shoes she would have landed like a cat—but the high pumps made her slip" and so she winds herself. Having torn the hem of the evening dress and lost her tiara, she puts her old shorts and shirt back on, although "she was too big to wear shorts anymore after this" (*H* 105). It becomes painfully clear that womanhood, here signaled by dress, is a hindrance to the hopes and plans of the young tomboys.

For the young girls, then, femininity emerges as a stranger mode of being than tomboyhood. While femininity makes Mick feel different from herself (*H* 97), Frankie is unable to perform it properly and, even if unwittingly, she makes a mockery of ideal womanhood. In this way, both texts construct the southern ideal of femininity as, ironically, *freakish*. The young girl's developing body and emerging sexuality herald the onset of a freakish womanliness, and her unease in the face of such developments comes to the fore as sexual differences become more marked in the eroticization of the body's surfaces: the boy's flaccid and erect penis, and the girl's budding breasts. So, in *The Heart Is a Lonely Hunter* Mick picks "at the front of her blouse to keep the cloth from rubbing the new, tender nipples beginning to come out on her breast" (29).

Mick Kelly's graffiti on the walls of a deserted house captures in essence the emerging eroticization of the youthful female body. In bold red and green chalk letters, she writes "a very bad word—PUSSY" (*H* 36–37). This graffiti reveals that Mick is alert to social constructions and perceptions of women as sex objects, whose sole function is a sexual one. It is no wonder the young girls fearfully consider their changing bodies as freakish, for femaleness frequently loses any capacity for alternative conceptualization beyond (male) obscenity.

The adolescents' fear wrought by the visibly changing pubertal body surfaces in McCullers's texts in those moments where the visceral manifests itself externally for all the world to see. In the short story "Like That" (*Mortgaged Heart*), for example, when eighteen-year-old Sis starts to menstruate, the narrator, Sis's nameless younger sister, exclaims: "'It shows. . . . It does too!' [Sis] had on a sweater and a blue pleated skirt and she was so skinny all over that it did show a little. 'Anybody can tell. Right off the bat. Just to look at you anybody can tell. . . . It looks terrible. I wouldn't ever be like that. It shows and everything'" (83). This passage clearly presents menstruation as freakish in both its visibility and unsight-

liness. It is not difficult to see the onset of menstruation as a terrifying event that signals to the world, and to the young woman, the arrival of a freakish womanhood.

For Mick Kelly, it is the loss of her virginity, again conjuring up the image of indelibly staining blood, which she understands as a visible marker of her entry to womanhood. Wondering if anyone can tell that she is no longer a virgin after her first sexual encounter with Harry Minowitz, she asks him: "'Tell me. Can you look at me and see the difference?' Harry watched her face for a long time and nodded that he could" (*H* 242). Subsequently, when Mick goes home to her family, "she had expected them to move back when they saw her and stand around in a circle and look. But they just glanced at her. She sat down at the table and waited. . . . Nobody noticed her." Eventually Mick asks Portia if she is able to "notice anything different": "'Sure I notice, Hon. . . . Just take a little grease and rub it on your face. . . . They say grease is the best thing for bad sunburn.' She [Mick] stood by herself in the back yard. . . . It was almost worse this way. Maybe she would feel better if they could look at her and tell. If they knew" (*H* 244–45).[4]

These examples suggest that the young women's pubertal bodies are burdensome because of their visibility, and are seemingly inscribed with inner secrets signaling the onset of what must seem like the "sentence" of womanhood. As a result, the young girls are clearly marked as different—different from what they once were, and different from the models of ideal womanhood displayed before them, as epitomized by the demure clubhouse members in *The Member of the Wedding*.

Mick's dis-ease after the loss of her virginity is apparent in the following traumatic image: "It was like her head was broke off from her body and thrown away" (*H* 241). This description anticipates Hélène Cixous's claim that decapitation is the female equivalent of male castration: "[I]f masculinity is culturally ordered by the castration complex, . . . the backlash . . . on women of this castration anxiety is its displacement as decapitation, execution, of woman, as loss of head" (43).[5] Mick's loss of virginity, and thus of girlhood, signals the loss of power that is inherent in southern womanhood. A taste of what is in store for her as a woman occurs when, as mother-substitute, she must baby-sit her younger brothers. Biff Brannon, the owner of the New York Café, watches Mick "pulling a couple of

snotty babies in a wagon. But if she wasn't nursing or trying to keep up with the bigger ones, she was by herself" (*H* 20). Loss of virginity, together with the graffiti "PUSSY" and surrogate motherhood, draw attention to women's ideal function as solely reproductive.

The adolescent girls' fear or bewilderment in the face of a mutating body and developing sexuality, along with their concomitant feelings of strangeness, also appears in McCullers's short story "Wunderkind" (*Mortgaged Heart*, also in M). Alice Hall Petry is right to posit as central to the story the subtle sexual relationship between the young girl, Frances, and her piano teacher, Mr. Bilderbach (31–39). Frances is on the threshold of an awakening and disturbing sexuality. Accordingly, the language in the story resonates with an aggressive sexual energy: the music is "urging violently" (90), Bilderbach's veins throb, "the muscles of his strong thighs [strain] under the cloth of his trousers" (101), and Frances feels "that if he looked at her much longer her hands might tremble" (87). Overwhelmed, she rejects adulthood as defined in terms of sexual activity and response and, bursting from Bilderbach's music studio, she attempts a return to childhood: she "turned in the wrong direction, and hurried down the street that had become confused with noise and bicycles and the games of other children" (99).

Frankie, like Frances, also fails to understand adult sexuality. The only sex education she receives is when she witnesses the household boarders' "common fit" (M 50) and "the unknown sin that [Barney MacKean] had shown her" in the MacKeans' garage (M 91). These encounters with sexuality culminate in Frankie's "date" with the soldier, which goes disastrously wrong when he attempts to rape her upstairs in the Blue Moon Café. For Frankie, his unwelcome advance is "like a minute in the fair Crazy-House, or the real Milledgeville" (M 161), which leaves "disgust in her mouth" (M 164). Frankie's allusion to the Crazy-House neatly captures the sexual distress also experienced by Mick and Frances.

Thus, whichever path the adolescent girls travel down—either tomboyishness or culturally sanctioned femininity—they are socially perceived, and perceive themselves, as "odd." The following lines from McCullers's poem "Saraband" suggest Mick's and Frankie's subsequent sense of claustrophobia, restlessness, and frustration: "Bewildered by the paradox of all your musts / Turning from horizon to horizon, noonday to dusk" (*Mort-*

gaged Heart 300). In *The Member of the Wedding,* Berenice describes such confinement as being "caught." When Frankie, whom McCullers frequently describes in terms of tightness,[6] voices her dreams of traveling the world in search of adventure, Berenice responds: "We all of us somehow caught. We born this way or that way and we don't know why. . . . And maybe we wants to widen and bust free. But no matter what we do we still caught" (141).[7]

The all-pervasive atmosphere of claustrophobia in both *The Heart Is a Lonely Hunter* and *The Member of the Wedding* manifests itself in the many captivity tropes, from ostensibly benign places of confinement—a house, a room, a small town—to the more sinister prisons and asylums that feature so often in McCullers's fiction. Westling argues that in the writings of Welty, Flannery O'Connor, and McCullers, place functions "as an index of feminine identity" to register the "confinement which has been woman's traditional lot" (178–80). However, "McCullers's landscapes are much more confined than those of either Welty or O'Connor, for action is almost always limited to one or at most a few interiors" (6). Seemingly trapped in the kitchen or in the small-town streets, Frankie even envies the prisoners in the town jail, for "[i]t was better to be in a jail where you could bang the walls than in a jail you could not see" (*M* 84).

Heat adds to the girls' sense of suffocation: both Mick's and Frankie's narratives take place in hot southern summers, and for Frankie, heat becomes clearly associated with entrapment when she observes that "the bars of sunlight crossed the back yard like the bars of a bright strange jail" (*M* 95).[8] In contrast to the oppressive heat of their hometowns, both Mick and Frankie dream of the cool of other climes: for Frankie, this is Alaska; for Mick, Switzerland. Heat, then, intensifies the already stifling atmosphere created by the streets of the monotonous summer southern towns and the enclosed spaces such as the ubiquitous kitchens or cafés the tomboys frequent.

Mick Kelly describes her captivity as "like the ceiling was slowly pressing down towards her face" (*H* 273). She senses such claustrophobia earlier in the novel when she dreams that she is "swimming through great crowds of people. . . . The biggest crowd in the world. And sometimes . . . I'm knocking them all down . . . —and other times I'm on the ground and people are trompling all over me" (*H* 38–39). Consequently, she feels that "she could knock down all the walls of the house and then march through the streets as a big giant" (*H* 220). Frankie, in *her* desire to "bust free," "did things and got herself into real trouble. She broke the law. And once having become a criminal, she broke the law again, and then again" (*M* 33). And so, like Huck Finn, she yearns "to light out," "for South America or Hollywood or New York City" (*M* 34).

Both Mick's and Frankie's experience of being "caught" in the cross fire of restrictive adult expectations and youthful aspirations causes them to angrily "freak out," as their masochistic violence suggests. For example, in *The Member of the Wedding,* while Berenice tells Frankie of her four ex-husbands, Frankie "slices waxy yellow rinds from the bottoms of her feet" (36). And recalling "the unknown sin" with Barney MacKean, Frankie "shook herself hard and began smashing peas and rice together on her plate" (99). It seems that it is marriage, the destiny of every good girl, and sexual relations that cause Frankie to lash out masochistically in rage and rebellion.

Mick Kelly's masochistic urges emerge with specifically sexual overtones. After the disaster of her prom party, where she is unable to perform femininity "properly," she roams the nighttime streets to "this house where she had gone so many times this summer" in order to listen to the radio (*H* 106). Listening to a Beethoven symphony, "[s]he sat with her arms held tight around her legs, biting her salty knees very hard." When the music stops, "[s]uddenly Mick began hitting her thigh with her fists. . . . But she could not feel this hard enough. She grabbed a handful of [rocks] and began scraping them up and down on the same spot until her hand was bloody. . . . With the fiery hurt in her leg she felt better. She was limp on the wet grass" (*H* 108).[9] Mick's masochism is not merely a process of catharsis in an environment of repression and captivity. Rather, the sexual nature of Mick's freaking out once more points to an emerging sexuality at odds with the image of the sexually disinterested southern lady.

Both texts consolidate Mick's and Frankie's difference by representing them as freak-like, as well as by directly associating Frankie with real-life physical freaks on her visit to the freak show at the Chattahoochee Exposition. Here on display are the Giant, the Fat Lady, the Midget, the Wild Nigger, the Pin Head, the Alligator Boy, and the Half-Man Half-

Woman. Before this visit, Frankie already has some sense of her freakishness. One day she looks in the "watery kitchen mirror. . . . The reflection in the glass was warped and crooked, but Frankie knew well what she looked like": "a big freak" (M 8–9). Already sensing her association with freaks, then, when she visits the fair, "[s]he was afraid of all the Freaks, for it seemed to her that they had looked at her in a secret way and tried to connect their eyes with hers, as though to say: we know you" (M 27).[10]

Fiedler claims that Frankie's encounter with the freaks reveals "the secret self" (*Freaks* 18).[11] However, he misses the important point that identification of self with freakdom is a social practice, not an inherent condition. Accordingly, Robert Bogdan writes that "'[f]reak' is not a quality that belongs to the person on display. It is something we created: a perspective, a set of practices—a social construction" (xi). With regard to *The Member of the Wedding*, we can conclude that Frankie's fear of the freaks is a consequence of her incorporation of commonly held social mores and standards.

We might define the freak, like the adolescent, according to physical distortion and in opposition to the "normal" body. One consequence is that the sight or presence of freaks enables the perception of one's own self as normal. More specifically, the physical distortion of the freak (and its contingency based on looking) means that it falls into the realm of spectacle. Susan Stewart explores structures of looking in her significant study, *On Longing*, to claim that "the spectacle assumes that the object is blinded; only the audience sees." She argues that it is the distance between the viewer and the freak-object that allows the viewer to avoid the "contamination" of the object on display (108–9). This assures viewers of their normalcy just as the freak becomes "caught" in their static and distanced gaze.

Stewart also makes the important point that the history of the freak is inextricably bound up with its capture in the dynamics of spectacle: "From Hellenistic times through the Middle Ages and the Renaissance, dwarfs, midgets, and occasionally gigantic figures were kept as accouterments of court life, as entertainers and pets. In the eighteenth century such figures were put on display in public taverns" (108). She takes Gulliver's adventures in Brobdingnag as an example: "[H]e is first kept in a box and exhibited on market days and in taverns; later he is rescued by an invitation to serve at court. The Queen . . . takes him on as a human pet or doll" (110).[12] In this regard, then, the spectacle of the freaks well suggests the experience of strangeness, visibility, and capture that Frankie and Mick undergo.

It is the dynamics of *looking* in the freak spectacle that thus ideally assign self and other as normal and freakish, respectively. In a similar formulation, Michel Foucault claims that in the relationship between networks of power and individuals, the visibility of the latter "assures the hold of the power that is exercised over them. It is the fact of being constantly seen, of being able always to be seen, that maintains the disciplined individual in his subjection" (*Reader* 199). In *The Member of the Wedding,* the Half-Man Half-Woman, whose "eyes were strange," suggests the blindness or unseeingness involved in the "disciplining" of the freak.

However, when Frankie views the freaks at the exposition, they hold her in their "long Freak eyes" (M 27). The presumed distance between spectator and spectacle along with the presumed blindness of the object falls away, marking Frankie as freakish. She becomes contaminated by the closeness of the freaks' gaze. In this way, the supposed demarcation between freak-other and normal-self, the ideal dynamic of the freak spectacle, fails to confirm the normalcy of Frankie the spectator. She becomes one of the freaks because, being *different,* she is *like* them.

The Member of the Wedding as well as *The Heart Is a Lonely Hunter* further construct Frankie and Mick as freakish through less overt associations: with the freaks whom Frankie sees at the sideshow, particularly the Pin Head, the Giant, and the Half-Man Half-Woman. For example, on one occasion, Frankie resembles the Pin Head who has "a shrunken head no larger than an orange, which was shaved except for one lock tied with a pink bow at the top" (M 27). Berenice describes Frankie in her wedding outfit in similar terms: "You had all your hair shaved off like a convict, and now you tie a silver ribbon around this head without any hair. It just looks peculiar" (M 106).

Mick and Frankie are also giant-like.[13] Accordingly, Frankie is "five feet five and three-quarter inches tall and wore a number seven shoe. In the past year she had grown four inches. . . . If she reached her height on her eighteenth birthday, she had five and one-sixth growing years ahead of her. Therefore . . . she would grow to be over nine feet tall" (*M* 25). When Frankie worries that "a lady who is over nine feet tall . . . would be a Freak," Berenice assures her that marriage will stunt her growth. But Frankie is caught in a predicament, for she doubts if freaks "ever get married or go to a wedding" (*M* 27). As Berenice also points out, it is the naturally endowed female, such as the "small and pretty" Janice (*M* 37–38), who is more likely marriage material.

Mick Kelly is even taller than Frankie and, like her, experiences her height as a hindrance to social poise and acceptance. She is "[f]ive feet six inches tall and a hundred and three pounds, and she was only thirteen. Every kid at the party was a runt beside her. No boy wanted to prom with a girl so much taller than him. But maybe cigarettes would help stunt the rest of her growth" (*H* 101). Harry Minowitz only fans Mick's anxiety about her height: "'Once I saw a lady at the fair who was eight and a half feet tall. But you probably won't grow that big'" (*H* 101).

In addition, the healthy appetites of both girls further their resemblance to the giants (*H* 144; *M* 29, 34, 126). Both Portia, the Kellys' cook, and Berenice warn Mick (*H* 44) and Frankie (*M* 126), respectively, to cut down on their food intake. Greediness is unladylike and may increase their already freakish height. In the same way that McCullers portrays the adolescent body, the giant is a "violator of boundary and rule," presenting "a physical world of disorder and disproportion" (Stewart 73–74).

The gigantic proportions of Mick and Frankie conflict with the more appropriate, delicate height of "ladies." This contrast becomes clear when we compare the adolescent girls with Janice, mentioned above, and the doll-like Baby Wilson of *The Heart Is a Lonely Hunter*. Baby, Biff Brannon's niece, "looked like a fairy . . . with a little pink-gauze skirt, . . . and even a little pink pocket-book . . . she was . . . so small" (147). This emphasis on petiteness enshrines the feminine image of the domesticated "little woman," in contrast with the unbridled giant with whom Mick and Frankie are indirectly compared.[14]

Finally, Mick and Frankie resemble the Half-Man Half-Woman of the sideshow, that "morphidite and a miracle of science" (*M* 27). The phrase "miracle of science" further enhances the imprisoning dynamics of the spectacle that Stewart outlines. The scientific discourses that played an important role in the creation of the category of freak, particularly in the nineteenth century, produced freaks as subhuman specimens, not far removed from animals. In this way, science "legitimated the public's voyeuristic interest in freak exhibits" (Weinstock 329).

More significantly, Mick and Frankie are comparable with the double-gendered hermaphrodite because of their blurring of gendered appearance and masculine identification. Described as "divided completely in half—the left side was a man and the right side a woman. The costume on the left was a leopard skin and on the right side a brassiere and spangled skirt. Half the face was dark-bearded and the other half bright glazed with paint" (M 27), not only does the Half-Man Half-Woman signal gender confusion but also the confounding of illusion and reality. It is worth noting that the *illusion* of the Half-Man Half-Woman is maintained by the focus on costume rather than anatomy, again stressing that gender is something to be put on, just as Mick's and Frankie's femininity is signaled by costume. Thus, dependence on illusion and suspension of disbelief further underscores the ambiguous gender of the hermaphrodite.

The hermaphrodite is a powerful and disturbing image with which to express adolescent sexual distress and gender confusion. Furthermore, as Westling notes, other images of androgyny throughout *The Member of the Wedding* "are placed in a negative frame, for the entire novel's movement is towards Frankie's ultimate submission to the inexorable demand that she accept her sex as female" (127).[15] Frankie's fear of all the freaks expresses an acknowledgment of the socially perceived oddness of her tomboy status, which exceeds the limits of "proper" feminine identity.

Thus, in opposing the ideal of woman, the tomboys are marked as freaks. It seems that maturity involves the "ability to believe oneself normal" and the other as freakish (Fiedler, *Freaks* 31). The freak is thus a fruitful and appropriate trope for the expression of the adolescent experience of otherness and perplexity, for it highlights the manner in which normative gender politics statically contain and mark out the young tomboys in oddness. Just as significantly, images of freakishness associated with "normal" femininity also signal that all is not well in the realm of identity politics.

Freakishness, then, is a social construction and is thus contingent on ways of reading. The implication is that freak-identification is open to anyone, not just to the narrowly defined sideshow freak: "In reality, everyone is a freak because no human can cram her/himself into the narrow space that is the state of normalcy" (Segrest 25).[16] Accordingly, the rest of this chapter will posit a new reading of the freak-adolescent in terms of the challenge it provides to socially sanctioned identity formation. This is a more productive way of reading McCullers's adolescents, rather than simply consigning them to freakdom or rejecting the term altogether, which, as already noted, several feminist readers of McCullers's works have done.

So far, I have made links between the young adolescent girls and freakishness: in sum, both defy the "normal" body through their own physical distortion. There is, however, one major difference in McCullers's representation of Mick and Frankie and the category of freak, and this is what I suggest is a question of *movement:* the girls have more in common with the mutable world of the grotesque than with the stasis that defines the figure of the freak. The issue of age provides a good example of this and is a marker crucial to any discussion of McCullers's adolescents. Although we never really know the ages of the freaks who appear in *The Member of the Wedding,* we can infer from their titles that they are at least meant to represent *either* youth *or* old age: the Midget, the Pin Head girl, and the Alligator Boy signal youth; the Giant, the Fat Lady, and the Half-Man Half-Woman signal adulthood. However, although freaks can be any age, they always remain either the Alligator *Boy* or the Fat *Lady*, regardless of the real age of the freak performer. Thus, the apparently ageless immutability of freakishness further emphasizes it as a world of stasis or capture.

In strict contrast, Mick and Frankie, who are on the threshold of maturity, hover between childhood and adulthood. Unsurprisingly, *The Heart Is a Lonely Hunter* and *The Member of the Wedding* contain many images of their adolescent protagonists standing in doorways. In fact, the very first image of Mick in *The Heart Is a Lonely Hunter* is of her standing

in a doorway (20).[17] As in *The Heart Is a Lonely Hunter, The Member of the Wedding* immediately presents Frankie as someone "who hung around in doorways" (7).[18] Later, Frankie recounts her dream to the clairvoyant Big Mama: "'[T]here was a door. . . . I was just looking at it and while I watched, it began slowly to open. And it made me feel funny and I woke up.'" Significantly, Big Mama interprets the dream as signaling the arrival of change in Frankie's life (149–50).[19]

Unlike the sideshow freaks, the girls are not fixed in regard to age: they are neither children nor adults. Rather, Mick and Frankie have more in common with what Russo has termed the "intergenerational grotesque," recalling the Bakhtinian grotesque body, which is a cyclically aging body for, although it is founded on the figures of the senile old hags, these hags are *pregnant*. In this way, aging is connected to death and rebirth and is thus a productive, albeit agonizing, process.

Mick and Frankie are similarly on the threshold of appropriate gender identification; they are neither masculine nor feminine but resemble the hermaphroditic Half-Man Half-Woman. In the earlier discussion of the Half-Man Half-Woman of *The Member of the Wedding,* I showed how the freakish hermaphrodite challenges notions of a singly and statically gendered body in this way.

Gender confusion is also apparent in the grotesque world of *Rabelais and His World.* Although the social reality of carnival is apparently reserved for men alone (23), the grotesque body is nonetheless founded on the image of woman. In another twist, Bakhtin describes the Rabelaisian body elsewhere as an androgyne: "a man's body with two heads . . . a brace of sexual organs, male and female" (323), a figure difficult to classify in terms of gender. This combination of images—the pregnant hag and the androgyne—suggests the amorphousness of the gendered body. Thus, while indeterminate gendering is obviously definitive of the freakish, it is also an element that is basic to the grotesque, as well as to McCullers's portrayal of Mick and Frankie.

Importantly, gender is inextricably entwined with age for both Mick and Frankie. For the girl to become a woman, she must shed her boyishness.[20] So, for example, Frankie's purchase of the orange satin dress to wear to her brother's wedding symbolizes her bid to assume adulthood. And in *The Heart Is a Lonely Hunter,* by the end of the prom party and her attempts at dressing as a grownup, Mick reverts to youth, that is, to her boyishness, symbolized by her donning of shorts and sneakers.

It is perhaps Frankie's name changes that best exemplify the tomboys' shift in gender identification. Defying Berenice's maxim that "things accumulate around your name. . . . [Y]ou just can't jump out of your name and escape like that" (M 34), the tomboy Frankie becomes the feminine "F. Jasmine" who dreams of stardom, wants to wear an orange satin evening dress, and drowns herself in Sweet Serenade perfume because the neighborhood children tell her she smells. Finally, Frankie becomes the sensible Frances (Frankie's real name) and leads an appropriately sensible "daytime" life (M 189).

Thus, throughout the novel, Frankie, like Mick, fluctuates between boyishness and girlishness, a movement epitomized in her vision of a better world where "people could instantly change back and forth from boys to girls, whichever way they felt like and wanted" (M 16). This image recalls to some extent the Half-Man Half-Woman of the Chattahoochee Exposition. Similarly, the categories of age and gender cannot contain the adolescent, for thresholds have no bounds. McCullers's representations of liminal, adolescent subjectivity promise becoming, or at least *potential*, and so puncture the overwhelming entrapment of freak identity. The trope of the unfinished, which is associated with Mick and Frankie, only serves to underscore this promise. To be unfinished is to participate in an open-ended subjectivity. In *Rabelais and His World*, Bakhtin writes that the grotesque body "is not a closed, completed unit; it is unfinished, outgrows itself, transgresses its own limits. . . . This is the ever unfinished, ever creating body" (25–26). Likewise, the young girls of *The Heart Is a Lonely Hunter* and *The Member of the Wedding* are unfinished, and this is an epithet Frankie herself uses (M 32) and at least invokes: the world is "cracked and loose" (M 30, 47, 142–43) and she is "unjoined" (M 7).

Images of "unfinishedness" or an incompleteness abound in *The Member of the Wedding*, particularly in references to unfinished music. Early on in the novel, Frankie hears "[f]rom somewhere far away . . . the sound of whistling, and it was a grieving August song that did not end" (25).[21] In the short story "The Sojourner," John himself "reads" the image of unfinished music: "There's nothing that makes you so aware of the improvisation of human existence as a song unfinished" (B 129). The nature of the unfinished also occurs in a beautiful image when Frankie recalls the clairvoyant Big Mama's description of Honey Brown: "She said he was a boy God had not finished. The Creator had withdrawn His hand from him too soon. God had not finished him, and so he had to go around doing one thing and then another to finish himself up" (M 151).

Although the unfinished state often causes pain—Frankie feels "lost" (M 55), sad and "jittery" (M 103), and Honey, who is "left eternally unsatisfied" (M 152), is sentenced to a chain gang for a drugstore robbery—I suggest that such images open the way for becomings, reflecting McCullers's own belief that "[a]ny growing thing must go through awkward stages" (*Mortgaged Heart* 270). Thus, the tropes of the threshold and the unfinished provide ways of thinking about McCullers's freak-adolescents other than in terms of some individual malfunction or of their struggle to achieve "normal" adulthood. Rather, such tropes promise becoming. Because Mick and Frankie, and all adolescents, are liminal and so unfinished, they embody this form of continuous, ever-creating "becoming," and this is something not accounted for in the identification of the adolescents with the sideshow freaks. The process of becoming is also what defines the Rabelaisian grotesque body: it "is not concerned with a completed and closed body but with the one that is born, which is in the stage of becoming" (*Rabelais* 179). To clarify further, for Bakhtin, becoming is defined not only against stable and singular identity but also against the "single crisis of rebirth" (Morson and Emerson 382). Bakhtin's concept of becoming can lead to a fuller understanding of McCullers's representation of adolescents in their revolutionary challenge to both static *and* evolutionary identity.

The attempt to move beyond restrictive bounds of classical, "finished" identity is reflected in both Mick's and Frankie's representation as giants. The giant is "an essentially grotesque image" (Bakhtin, *Rabelais* 341) that challenges configurations of the body as a closed and finished system; the giant grows beyond what is culturally deemed natural and normal and could be said to represent the possibility of a new subjectivity.

But it is perhaps Frankie's "we of me" fantasy—and the implicit fantasy of the "unnatural nuptials" (Deleuze and Guattari 273)—that most powerfully suggests becoming, or growth. Frankie plans to be a member of her brother's wedding in the hope of becoming a "we of me." Before she entertains this vision, she envies soldiers and even chain gangs for they "can say *we*" (M 52–53). Frankie, on the other hand, "was an *I* person who had to walk around and do things by herself. All other people had a *we* to claim, all others except her. . . . But the old Frankie had no *we* to claim, unless it would be the terrible summer *we* of her and John Henry and Berenice—and that was the last *we* in the world she wanted. Now all this was suddenly over with and changed. There was her brother and the bride, and it was as though when first she saw them something she had known inside of her: *They are the we of me*" (M 52–53). She quickly decides what she must do: "'After the wedding at Winter Hill, I'm going off with the two of them to whatever place that they will ever go. I'm going with them'" (M 56–57).

This passage has been read in various ways, most predominantly as either an incestuous or a homoerotic fantasy.[22] McCullers herself offers two quite different interpretations of the "we of me" fantasy, only fueling its puzzling nature. In her recently published memoir, *Illumination and Night Glare*, McCullers writes that while working on *The Member of the Wedding* she had an "illumination: 'Frankie is in love with the bride of her brother and wants to join the wedding,'" she declared to Gypsy Rose Lee (32). And in her essay "Loneliness . . . An American Malady," she explains, retrospectively, that Frankie's yearning to join the wedding reflects the universal need to belong: "After the [child's] first establishment of identity there comes the imperative need to lose this new-found sense of separateness and to belong to something larger and more powerful than the weak, lonely self" (*Mortgaged Heart* 265). Several readers have taken up this latter exposition of the passage to claim that "the underlying wish is to assuage the terror of separateness by regression to an undifferentiated state before there is an 'I'" (Dalsimer 21).[23] What such readings amount to is a conservative fantasy of fusion that is, in the end, statically enclosed. The process of becoming, on the other hand, is a continuous and arduous process of metamorphosis. That is to say, becoming a "we of me" carries within it the possibility of new selves and new relationships with other selves.

Frankie's two name changes, already mentioned as an example of the way the adolescent girl straddles childhood and womanhood, are also indicative of her attempt at becoming. Frankie chooses "Jasmine"—a suitably fanciful, romantic name—to participate in the wedding, since she

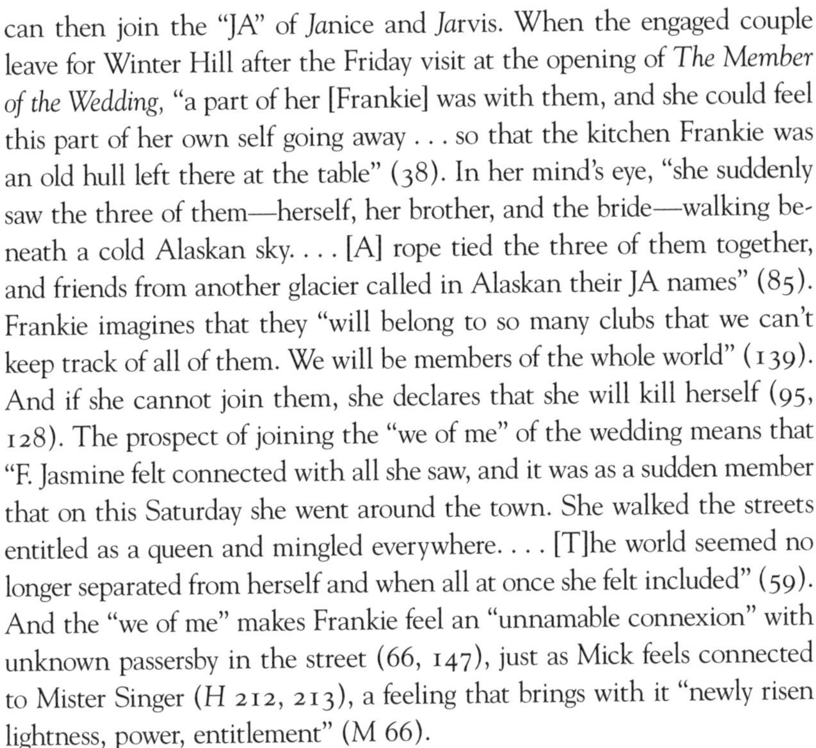

can then join the "JA" of *Ja*nice and *Ja*rvis. When the engaged couple leave for Winter Hill after the Friday visit at the opening of *The Member of the Wedding,* "a part of her [Frankie] was with them, and she could feel this part of her own self going away . . . so that the kitchen Frankie was an old hull left there at the table" (38). In her mind's eye, "she suddenly saw the three of them—herself, her brother, and the bride—walking beneath a cold Alaskan sky. . . . [A] rope tied the three of them together, and friends from another glacier called in Alaskan their JA names" (85). Frankie imagines that they "will belong to so many clubs that we can't keep track of all of them. We will be members of the whole world" (139). And if she cannot join them, she declares that she will kill herself (95, 128). The prospect of joining the "we of me" of the wedding means that "F. Jasmine felt connected with all she saw, and it was as a sudden member that on this Saturday she went around the town. She walked the streets entitled as a queen and mingled everywhere. . . . [T]he world seemed no longer separated from herself and when all at once she felt included" (59). And the "we of me" makes Frankie feel an "unnamable connexion" with unknown passersby in the street (66, 147), just as Mick feels connected to Mister Singer (*H* 212, 213), a feeling that brings with it "newly risen lightness, power, entitlement" (M 66).

Frankie's feeling of "connexion" recalls Bakhtin's description of the medieval carnival: "The individual feels that he is an indissoluble part of the collectivity, a member of the people's mass body. In this whole the individual body ceases to a certain extent to be itself; it is possible, so to say, to exchange bodies, to be renewed (through change of costume and mask). At the same time the people become aware of their sensual, material bodily unity and community" (*Rabelais* 255). In *The Member of the Wedding,* "connexion" or "material bodily unity" occurs most literally in an image when Frankie "decided to donate blood to the Red Cross; . . . her blood would be in the veins of Australians and Fighting French and Chinese, all over the whole world, and it would be as though she were close kin to all of these people" (31). Such a fantasy of becoming conflicts with configurations of Frankie's adolescent identity as simply caught, which suggests, rather, the finished identity of the sideshow freak. Another example of physical merging, this time with the cosmos, occurs in *The Heart Is a Lonely Hunter.*[24] Harry's vision of the afterlife is one in which "after you were dead and buried you changed to plants and fire and dirt and clouds and water. It took thousands of years and then finally you were a part of all the world. He said he thought it was better than being one single angel" (235).

In *The Heart Is a Lonely Hunter,* Mick articulates "connexion" in terms of a "bunch." Neither belonging to the Girl Scouts (20) nor having any friends at Vocational High, "she planned to be in a bunch almost as much as she thought of music" (95). Similarly, the adolescent Jester Clane, in *Clock Without Hands,* envies Sherman Pew's talk of the Golden Nigerian club, which attempted to vote "as a body" in the segregated South: "'I wish I had been there when you registered as a body,' Jester said wistfully. The phrase 'as a body' particularly appealed to him and heroic tears came suddenly to his eyes" (64). Like his adolescent counterparts, Harry, who is Jewish, also yearns to be a part of a "bunch" and admits that he once admired the Hitler Youth, "marching and singing songs and keeping step together. . . . All of them pledged to each other and with one leader. All of them with the same ideals." Harry's wonder is rapidly extinguished as he learns "'what was happening to the Jewish minorities. . . . I thought I was a Fascist. Of course later I found out I was different'" (*H* 217).

Both Frankie and Mick wish that *they* were different. In such a wish, they are expressing the desire to become, to metamorphose beyond types. Mick wants to be "foreign" like Mozart and Beethoven, who "spoke in a foreign language and lived in a foreign place" (*H* 106). She takes Spanish lessons, which are "grand" for they make "her feel like she'd been round a lot" (*H* 93). Similarly, Frankie wishes "'I was somebody else except me'" (M 12) and so she "walked all around . . . wearing her Mexican hat and the high-laced boots and a cowboy rope tied round her waist, she had gone around pretending to be Mexican. Me no speak English—Adios Buenos Noches—abla pokie peekie poo, she had jabbered in mock Mexican. . . . [W]hen the game was over, and she was home, there would come over her a cheated discontent" (M 73).

The grand dreams of both girls fortify their respective portrayals in terms of potential. Mick considers being an "inventor" of radios "the size of a green pea" or of "flying machines people could fasten on their backs";

or she plans perhaps to "make a large tunnel through the world to China" (*H* 34–35). And "more than anything else" she wants to learn the piano (*H* 39) in order to become "a great world-famous composer. She would have a whole symphony orchestra and conduct all of her music herself" (*H* 211). Mick's plans take place in the "inside room," an immanent theater she constructs to act out possible transformation.[25] Her dreams are no vain desires, evidenced by her decision to take mechanical shop over typing class and in her attempt to make a violin (*H* 43). Furthermore, she spends her lunch money on piano lessons from a young school friend, Delores Brown, which makes her "very hungry all through the day" (*H* 144). Once she is virtually forced to work at Woolworth's, she plans "to set aside a little for a second-hand piano" (*H* 307).

Frankie also has big plans and she yearns to "light out and never see this town again" (M 12). Like Mick (*H* 215), Frankie wishes to join the war, to either fly airplanes or join the Marines (M 30–31). Or perhaps she "would go on to Hollywood and write shows and get a job as a movie starlet—or, if worse came to worse, even act in comedies" (M 175). And later, she decides she will become "a great poet—or else the foremost authority on radar" (M 186). Like her name changes, Frankie's running away from home is an attempt at self-transformation. These may only be typical adolescent dreams, but at least Mick and Frankie *do* dream, *do* imagine other possibilities of being, and, as noted, Mick *does* try to make her dreams come true.

All these associations of adolescence with becoming a "we of me" are typical of the Rabelaisian grotesque body, a body that "leads men out of the confines of the apparent (false) unity, of the indisputable and stable" (*Rabelais* 48). More mobile or plastic than the type of sideshow freak, the Bakhtinian concept of the grotesque enables a redefinition, or at least a renegotiation, of McCullers's vision of adolescent subjectivity.

The "lines of flight," or potential, which define becoming, surface in tropes of actual flight that occur regularly in McCullers's fiction.[26] James Johnson claims that flight, an important image in the novels of adolescence in the decades following the 1930s, represents the adolescent "hero's" desire for escape from the realization of "one's bodily and spiritual isolation." In his brief discussion of *The Member of the Wedding*, he writes

that "Frankie ran away to avoid facing her humiliation," following the "nightmare" of the wedding (7). But the more literal images of flight that are ubiquitous in McCullers's novels of adolescence might suggest not merely escape but rather transformation. Flight suggests liminality (it occurs on the threshold of heaven and earth) and is compatible with the movement of becoming, which I have traced in both *The Heart Is a Lonely Hunter* and *The Member of the Wedding.*

In her discussion of flight, Mary Russo links the boyishness of Amelia Earhart with "aeriality" to suggest that flight is symbolic of (virile) activity and danger: as "the fantasy of a femininity which defies the limits of the body, especially the female body" (44),[27] flight bears within it the potential for testing limits and stepping out-of-bounds. Perhaps it is no coincidence that when the tomboy Mick decides that she will one day invent "flying machines," she is standing on the roof of an empty house, with her arms spread out "like wings" (*H* 33–34). It is through such an image of aeriality that Mick experiences lines of flight. Frankie's dreams also involve flight. She plans an ideal world where everyone is entitled to "an aeroplane and a motorcycle" (M 115), and she dreams of "flying aeroplanes and winning gold medals for bravery" in the war (M 31).

Although Russo suggests that flight is "the fantasy of a femininity," in McCullers's writings, the fantasy of flight is not projected by the girls alone. Jester Clane, in *Clock Without Hands,* believes, like Frankie, that everyone should be able to fly and own a plane (69). In "Author's Outline of 'The Mute'" (in *Mortgaged Heart*), both Mick and Harry West (who becomes Harry Minowitz in *The Heart Is a Lonely Hunter*) are "made restless by an abundance of undirected energy. In the spring they try to construct a glider together in the Kellys' backyard, and although because of inadequate materials they can never get the contraption to fly, they work at it very hard together" (140–41). The glider, which suggests the "expectancy" of a journey, is also an important image in "Untitled Piece," where the young boy, Andrew, and his younger sister, Sara, "read about gliders in a science magazine . . . and immediately they begin to build one in their back yard" (112). "It was as though they had never wanted anything except this glider and its flight from the earth up toward the hot blue sky" (113). However, Sara and Andrew crash the glider; like Mick and Andrew in the "Outline," their lines of flight are eventually obstructed.

RISKING "FEMALE LIMITS"

There is always an immanent risk in flight, which the Greeks called hybris and which the fateful flight of Icarus epitomizes. In McCullers's novels, the painful descriptions of the unfinished are indicative of the notion of risk, the consequences of which arise in Mick's paintings of failed flight: a painting titled *Sea Gull with Back Broken in Storm,* and one illustrating "an airplane crashing down and people jumping out to save themselves" (*H* 42). Again, up on the rooftop, "where everybody wanted to stand," Mick feels that "[t]here was something about getting to the very top that gave you a wild feeling and made you want to yell or sing or raise up your arms and fly." However, she also acknowledges the risk involved: "[I]f you lost grip and rolled off the edge it would kill you." So, Mick climbs down and as she well knows, "coming down is the hardest part of any climbing" (*H* 33–36).[28]

On the one hand, then, McCullers's texts construct adolescent subjectivity in the grotesque realm of becoming, providing a challenge to normative identity conceived as a static and finished whole. Mick Kelly and Frankie Addams testify to the potential of the process of becoming. On the other hand, however, McCullers's texts warn of the dangers of "flights of fancy." The risk has to do with overstepping the mark, of not toeing the line when it comes to "appropriate" gender performance. Those who fail to conform to strictly demarcated gender identity, organized along an axis of masculine/male and feminine/female, are castigated and ostracized by disciplinary measures. This is the warning McCullers's novels of adolescence would seem to issue in regard to an experimental adolescent subjectivity that enacts other, grotesque ways of being.

Some commentators consider the plight of Mick and Frankie at the end of their respective stories as a victory of socialization,[29] while others lament the girls' unfulfilled dreams.[30] Most readers agree that the adolescents surrender their rebellious becoming. Having strongly hinted at other possible subjectivities, Mick and Frankie, to some extent, *are* forced to surrender to the confines of conformity, to a restricted identity, as they take up the appropriate socially assigned roles of womanliness.

The concluding moments of *The Member of the Wedding* reveal Frankie's attempts to conform. Frankie is in the kitchen—now significantly whitewashed of the "queer drawings" (14) that once "gave the kitchen a crazy look" (10)—making "the sandwiches, cutting them into fancy shapes and taking great pains—for Mary Littlejohn was coming at five o'clock" (185). Perhaps Frankie's new friendship is the mark of her ultimate acceptance of womanhood.[31] The Frances of the end of *The Member of the Wedding* no longer sees "the earth as in the old days, cracked and loose and turning a thousand miles an hour; the earth was enormous and still and flat. Between herself and all the places there was a space like an enormous canyon she could not hope to bridge or cross. The plans for the movies or the Marines were only child plans that would never work" (83). The wedding itself turns out to be "as unmanaged as a nightmare" (168), and Frankie's old summertime fears and feeling of separateness return to engulf her: "[T]he failed wedding had quickened the fear to terror" (184). The movement or nomadism of the adolescent Frankie has become "still and flat," and her yearnings are now "only child plans." The text's portrayal of the new Frances recalls the sterile body of Renaissance representation that Bakhtin describes: "All signs of its [the grotesque body's] unfinished character, of its growth and proliferation were eliminated; its protuberances and offshoots were removed, its convexities (signs of new sprouts and buds) smoothed out, its apertures closed" (*Rabelais* 29). In a similar way, Frances has become a "molar identity." Gilles Deleuze and Félix Guattari warn that "it is dangerous to confine oneself to such a subject, which does not function without drying up a spring or stopping a flow. . . . Just as a dessicated [*sic*] child makes a much better child, there being no childhood flow emanating from it any longer" (276). Frances, then, is the "dried-up" version of Frankie and F. Jasmine, impeded by the demands of a restrictive social reality. This is anticipated to some extent when Frankie thinks to herself that it is "hard to argue with a known saying" (93). With all the talk around her of "little white boy beaus" and husbands, Frankie feels that Berenice is trying to "catch [her] by the collar, like the Law catches a no-good in the wrong, and jerk her back where she had started—back to the sad and crazy summer" (93–94).

Perhaps most significantly, Frankie no longer visits the freak show. On an earlier visit Frankie *identified* with the freaks. Maturity, as noted previously, supposedly entails a belief in one's normalcy and the casting of the other as freakish. As Frankie is forced to achieve acceptable femininity, she must now distance herself from such freak-identification. Frances, visiting the fair with Mary, "did not enter the Freak Pavilion, as Mrs Littlejohn said that it was morbid to gaze at freaks" (188).

Westling believes that Frankie "no longer feels any association with the freaks, for she is secure in her new feminine identity" (131). However, Frankie's avoidance of the Freak Pavilion may reveal, rather, the *fragility* of "normal" (in this case, "feminine") identity. A stable sense of a culturally sanctioned identity depends not just on the marked-off other as a measure against which to define "normality" but on the *exclusion* of that other. That the freak-other must be excluded only means that it is a powerful, potentially unsettling threat to stable identity.

Mick Kelly is also a victim of "desiccation," confined to the Woolworth's store, barred from the dynamism of her inside room, and deprived of "connexion" with Singer, who kills himself (*H* 248). Her dream of becoming the world's greatest composer is thwarted not only by the poverty of her family—which means she must contribute financially to their collective welfare—but also by her gender. Her education is not deemed as important as that of her male siblings. The new feminine attire Mick wears to work at Woolworth's is indicative of her recently acquired womanliness and the passing of youthful tomboyishness. Mick, like Frankie, must also feel caught, for Etta tells her "'[s]omeone ought to clamp down on you, Mick Kelly, and make you behave'" (*H* 41). Thus, Mick's and Frankie's fates testify to Westling's observation that "we find again and again the tomboy heroine suddenly confronted by society's demands that she subdue her behavior, accept the facts of adult sexuality that she has tried to deny, and start acting ladylike" (5).

Although both texts seem to represent the closure or desiccation of adolescent subjectivity, there are nonetheless aspects in the portrayal of Mick's and Frankie's rather mundane and unimaginative new adulthood that suggest that creative adolescent subjectivity does not end with adulthood. To locate these points, it is useful to return to the idea of flight and Russo's analysis of Amelia Earhart's stunt flying. Earhart represents the unprofessional stunt pilot, not the professional aviator, and as a stunt flier, she engages in improvisation (suggestive once more of the "unfinished"), which falls into "the realm of what is possible in the moment" (Russo 20–22). From this observation, Russo makes a useful distinction between "inherent possibility" and "future progress" (20–22), echoing Bakhtin's distinction between potential and simple rebirth. It is just such improvised, "inherent possibility" that McCullers's portrayals of the adolescents offer, even at the novels' conclusion. With regard to the four "friends" (Mick included) in *The Heart Is a Lonely Hunter*, McCullers, in her outline of "The Mute," writes: "Because of the essence of these people there is the feeling that, no matter how many times their efforts are wasted and their personal ideals are shown to be false, they will some day be united and they will come into their own" ("Author's Outline" 159). The vision of potential and hope or "inherent possibility" offered here is reflected in the conclusion of *The Heart Is a Lonely Hunter*. Although Mick feels her world collapse around her—brought on by the "two things she could never believe. That Mister Singer had killed himself and was dead. And that she was grown and had to work at Woolworth's" (306), as well as by the demise of her "inside room"—she is able to latch on to "some good." Considering the unlikely possibility of affording a secondhand piano, she nevertheless decides that

> maybe it would be true about the piano and turn out O. K. Maybe she would get a chance soon. Else what the hell good had it all been—the way she felt about her music and the plans she had made in the inside room? It had to be some good if anything made sense. And it was too and it was too and it was too and it was too. It was some good.
> All right!
> O.K.!
> Some good. (308)

The passage is worth quoting at length for its movement from a gentle sense of hope toward an insistent, determined, and necessary presence of possibility. As one reader notes, "[T]he phrase 'some good' represents the only kind of affirmation that matters: affirmation in the face of doubt, in the midst of pain, affirmation of life in the midst of living and producing life" (Budick 160).

I would suggest that the end of Frankie's story in *The Member of the Wedding* also offers "some good." Like Mick's world, Frankie's world has deteriorated: the wedding is a disaster, John Henry dies a horrifically painful death, and Berenice decides that "she might as well marry T. T." when Mister Addams and Frankie move to a new part of town (185). So, like Mick, Frankie starts on a new path. Although her grand dreams, like Mick's, may seem immediately thwarted, there are still hints of the imaginative little girl in the new Frances. She dreams of becoming a poet or an expert on radar and of traveling the world. Furthermore, the Catholic Mary Littlejohn has now replaced her freakish world, once signaled by her identification with the freaks and by the "we of me" of the crazily painted kitchen and its occupants. Although Berenice "was all of a sudden narrow-minded, saying that Roman Catholics worshipped Graven Images and wanted the Pope to rule the world[,] . . . for Frances this *difference* was a final touch of *strangeness*, silent terror, that completed the wonder of her love" (M 186–87, emphases added). The book ends with the arrival of Mary: "[T]he hush was shattered when, with an instant shock of happiness, she [Frankie] heard the ringing of the bell" (M 190). This irrepressible enthusiasm recalls the earlier Frankie, suggesting "that the old Frankie survives and may resurface" (Anandan 5).

These small concluding moments of McCullers's novels of adolescence intimate, with a gentle optimism, that Mick and Frankie will continue to emerge beyond the ending of their narratives. Although the image of the freak is useful in evoking adolescent dis-ease, the ways in which McCullers represents Mick Kelly and Frankie Addams go beyond an enclosed, caught identity. As I have shown, the categories of the grotesque and the freak do indeed overlap; I would suggest that the grotesque is an extension of the freak. In the end, the adolescents are then perhaps more properly figures of the grotesque and, consequently, point to the possibility of transformation or lines of flight that lie beyond the scope of the figure of the freak.

2
Queer Grotesques
The Heart Is a Lonely Hunter and *Reflections in a Golden Eye*

In the previous chapter's examination of freakish and grotesque adolescence, I argued that McCullers's portraits of the young girls point to a kind of becoming. In this chapter, I look at another type of freakish subjectivity—male homosexuality. To read homosexuality in *The Heart Is a Lonely Hunter* and *Reflections in a Golden Eye* is to stress again the radical nature of McCullers's vision, which embraces a particularly dynamic politics of the body. However, as I show, McCullers struggles to achieve this vision, as she confronts the still pressing problems of how to engage with the multiple meanings and possibilities of sexuality and gender. Freudian theory strongly influences McCullers's portraits of homosexual men, resulting, at times, in fairly orthodox portraits of homosexual desire, particularly in terms of the male homosexual's rejection of women, sexual impotence, narcissism, and decadence. On one level, I would suggest that McCullers relies on a more traditional configuration of homosexuality as a type of coding, allowing her to escape the censorship that disciplined the cultural scene of her times. However, on another level, that McCullers often uses damaging sexual stereotypes points to the difficulty of accessing a new language and a new body of images with which to represent grotesque desires. Her discernible struggle to depict a new configuration of homosexual desire, which is *productive*, testifies to the difficulty of her radical project and forces us to think more deeply about gender's complex relation to bodies and sexuality.

Although the term "homosexuality" was in circulation for almost fifty years before McCullers was writing her fiction,[1] she was the first southern novelist to write openly of homosexuality (Evans, *Carson McCullers* 60, with regard to *Reflections in a Golden Eye*). Nonetheless, she employs the term "homosexual" only rarely: with reference to Captain Penderton in her essay "The Flowering Dream: Notes on Writing," to Jester Clane in *Clock Without Hands*, and to Lily Mae Jenkins in both "Author's Outline of 'The Mute'" and *The Member of the Wedding*. More often, no doubt due to the social prescription of compulsory heterosexuality and the proscription of homosexual relationships at the time she wrote, McCullers's fictional treatment of such relationships is *coded* or implied through significant ellipses. It is what is *not* said that the reader must attend to in order to uncover inverted desire. Singer and Antonapoulos are mutes; Penderton is never named nor names himself as homosexual in *Reflections in a Golden Eye* itself. Instead, attentive readers are guided only with slight hints and clues into a labyrinthine world that undermines "normal" heterosexual relations.

The catchphrase "coming out of the closet" reflects the hidden status of homosexuality. Eve Kosofsky Sedgwick, who has coined the term "epistemology of the closet" to describe her theorization of male relationships, argues that binaries such as knowledge/ignorance, initiation/innocence, and, most significantly, secrecy/disclosure structure and underlie the supposed binary opposition homosexuality/heterosexuality (*Epistemology* 73).[2] And most historians of sexuality agree that silence has structured homosexuality from ancient Greece to the recent past.[3] It is a noisy silence insofar as it is common knowledge that "the love that dare not speak its name" is male same-sex passion. As long as homosexuality is considered an evil and/or illness, secrecy and silence are desirable. In cultural texts, then, it is often signs and symbols that stealthily suggest homosexuality.

Similarly, in McCullers's writings, "perverse" desire becomes most apparent through dreams and symbols and through its vicarious nature, as will become clearer in the course of this chapter. A pertinent example, however, concerns Alison Langdon's friend, Lieutenant Weincheck, in *Reflections in a Golden Eye*, who is nearly fifty years old and lives "in one of the apartment houses set aside for bachelor lieutenants, most of whom were just out of Westpoint." The officers, hearing the "naked melody" of Weincheck's violin playing, "scratch their heads and wink at each other" (38). This is a knowing wink, a secret signal, and the "knowing" reader must be "in the know" to know what the secret is.[4] In this way, the reader participates in "closet" machinations of secrecy/disclosure, ignorance/knowledge.

Accordingly, homosexual desire is never consummated in McCullers's works, perhaps due to the difficulty she had in writing about this at the time. Some readers claim that the sexual act occurs in *Reflections in a Golden Eye*, a book often compared to Herman Melville's *Billy Budd*.[5] In *Billy Budd*, Claggart, the ship's master-at-arms, begins to haunt Billy after the latter spills soup over him, seemingly indicative of a sexual exchange.[6] This reading could apply equally to the episode in *Reflections in a Golden Eye* where Private Williams spills coffee over Captain Penderton (4), setting off a chain of events similar to those in Melville's novella. But, however we are to read this most symbolic and debatable of gestures, the effects and affects of same-sex passion and the evocation of "impossible" desire are strongly present.

A crucial factor in McCullers's representations of grotesque desire is her own belief in the essential bisexuality of all human subjects and her frequent references to her own sexual and gender ambiguity: to repeat, she felt she was born a man and believed herself to be an invert (Carr, *The Lonely Hunter* 59, 167, see also 39).[7] Her stories and essays clearly reflect this belief in both her own bisexuality and the potential bisexuality of all human beings. For instance, in *The Heart Is a Lonely Hunter*, Biff Brannon claims that "[b]y nature all people are of both sexes" (119). Frankie Addams's and John Henry's respective visions of an ideal world in *The Member of the Wedding* also reflect a fluidity of sexed identity: "[Frankie] planned it so that people could change back and forth from boys and girls, whichever way they felt like it and wanted it. . . . And then John Henry would . . . think that people ought to be half boy and half girl" (116).

It is perhaps not surprising, then, that in McCullers's fiction, the normative love-object is not important; everyone is capable of making any object-choice. As the narrator explains in a discourse on love in *The Ballad of the Sad Café*, the "lover can be man, woman, child, or indeed any human creature on this earth." Similarly, "the beloved can also be of any description. The most outlandish people can be a stimulus for love" (33). And in the short story "A Tree, A Rock, A Cloud," an old tramp tells a young boy what he has discovered about "the science of love." He explains that before a man can love a woman, "the most dangerous and sacred experience on God's earth," he must "graduate from one thing to another": he must first love a tree, a rock, a cloud, until he "can love *anything*" (*B* 155–56, emphasis added). McCullers's major fiction also provides ample evidence for this reading of desire as mobile and nomadic, potentially alighting on any object of any kind. In *The Ballad of the Sad Café*, an Amazon loves a dwarf; in *The Heart Is a Lonely Hunter*, a deaf-mute loves a simpleton deaf-mute, and an "androgyne" desires an adolescent tomboy; in *Reflections in a Golden Eye*, an army captain desires his wife's lovers and then a "primitive" private. These couplings span both homosexual and heterosexual desire and thus play a significant part in McCullers's fictional strategy of resistance to oppressive configurations of normative sexuality.

In the following discussion of homosexual desire, I focus on the relationship of Singer and Antonapoulos,[8] and of Captain Penderton and Private Williams. I only make passing reference to Cousin Lymon and Marvin Macy of *The Ballad of the Sad Café*,[9] Bitsy Barlow of the short story "The Jockey" (*B* 103–9),[10] and Biff Brannon of *The Heart Is a Lonely Hunter*, as is necessary, since these figures do not add significantly to this discussion of homosexuality. Furthermore, the rather puzzling Biff Brannon, who is not, strictly speaking, homosexual, will appear in discussions of gender and androgyny in the subsequent chapters. Although this chapter does concentrate on McCullers's "queer" male grotesques, it will become clear that the tropes that construct homosexual identity are not in opposition to those that construct heterosexual identity. That is to say, there is no natural, fêted sexual position in McCullers's fictional worlds.[11]

I first examine the more orthodox and Freudian aspects of the texts' depiction of homosexuality, with regard to an aversion toward women and femininity more generally and its supposed links with impotence. However, by drawing on more recent revisions of Sigmund Freud, I then suggest that impotence in fact creates radical and unorthodox modes of pleasure, and by such extension of the body's practices and surfaces, McCullers's homosexual lovers are a part of the expansive world of the grotesque. Having picked up on the increasing subversiveness of McCullers's project, I extend this by looking at the ways her texts defy more traditional characterizations of homosexual men by undermining and dissolving such structural binaries as nature/culture and innocence/corruption. Finally, I return to the question of femininity and show how, although they are in flight from woman, the homosexual men in McCullers's texts have femininity work upon them as a powerful force. I would suggest that femininity, as much as masculinity, is a fiercely contested site in the struggle for expansive male identities.

FLIGHT FROM WOMAN

On first glance, masculinity and the world of men eclipse femininity and women in McCullers's fictional worlds.[12] When women register in McCullers's texts, they are either masculine,[13] adolescent tomboys,[14] absent mothers,[15] or dying or dead, often as a result of childbirth,[16] or they appear in the forms of *Reflections in a Golden Eye*'s silly Leonora Penderton or the hysterical Alison Langdon who chops off one of her nipples with garden shears. The feminine, then, if not entirely absent, is at least abjected from McCullers's fictional worlds except when it is assumed by men, a phenomenon I explore in later chapters.

In *The Ballad of the Sad Café*, for example, there are no female characters, save Miss Amelia, who herself is "like a man."[17] Amelia, raised by her father after the death of her mother in childbirth, refuses to treat female complaints in her role as a well-reputed healer. These "complaints" are what Private Williams terms "the bad sickness in women" (*R* 122), which the above examples of ailing femininity already suggest. As I will show, this fear of woman, specifically her genitalia and womb (the focus of "female complaints"), results in (male) hysteria. Miss Amelia, then, responds to women as a man might; that is to say, she even takes on a male neurosis.

Reflections in a Golden Eye also represents female bodies as a source of fear. Major Langdon associates femaleness, which is "altogether outside his control" (37), with morbidity. Twice we read of Private Williams's aversion to the female sex: "[B]rought up in a household exclusively male," Williams learns that "women carried in them a deadly and catching disease which made men blind, crippled, and doomed to hell" (23). Thus, Williams aligns women not only with sickness but also with contagion.

Consequently, "Private Williams had never willingly touched, or looked at, or spoken to a female since he was eight years old" (23). Recalling the time when he was ill in the hospital, he remembers how he shuddered when the female nurses "came near him, and he had lain for hours in misery rather than ask of them some service" (122).[18]

By contrast, Williams does not fear potential infection from female *animals*. He lovingly strokes the stomach of a pregnant mare and "stood for a time with his arms around her neck" (25). Thinking of the milking cow he bought when he was seventeen, he remembers how "[h]e would press his forehead against her warm flanks as he milked and talked to her in soft, urgent whispers" (30). It seems that for Williams, women are lower than the animals themselves. Women are the last link in the chain of being where, as McCullers notes in the poem "Love and the Rind of Time," "only a flicker of eternity divides us from unknowing beast" (*Mortgaged Heart* 296).

Like Private Williams, Captain Penderton also feels threatened by grotesque womanhood. Leonora, the Captain's sensuous and frisky young wife, is to him a "slattern" because of her "sudden excess of vigor." " 'You disgust me,' " he tells her. To taunt the Captain further, Leonora strips before him. Her naked body is "magnificent" with "a subtle quality of vibration," but Penderton experiences his wife's nudity as "a slap in the face" and threatens to kill her. Her nakedness reminds him of his impotence; that she becomes the castrator is emphasized in her question, " 'Son, have you ever been collared and dragged out in the street and thrashed by a naked woman?' " (*R* 17–19).

Biff Brannon similarly rejects any physical contact with women in *The Heart Is a Lonely Hunter*. While he entertains a strange fascination for the tomboy Mick and a fatherly affection for his niece, Baby Wilson, he tells his wife, Alice, that " '[n]ot but one woman I've ever known had this real kindness.' " So believing, "being around that woman [Alice] always made him different from his real self. It made him . . . common as she was" (17), which echoes Private Williams's belief that women are and have a contagious disease.

In the eyes of the Amazonian Miss Amelia, Private Williams, Captain Penderton, and Biff Brannon, then, womanhood is an awful and fearful thing. According to Freud in "Medusa's Head," such (usually male) fear arises from the "spectacle" of females' frightening genitals, which threatens castration while simultaneously revealing women's own castration. To illustrate his point, Freud recalls an instance in Rabelais's writings where "the Devil took to flight when the woman showed him her vulva" (273–74). For Rabelais, woman is "the bodily grave of man. . . . [S]he lifts her skirts and shows the parts through which everything passes (the underworld, the grave) and from which everything issues forth" (Bakhtin, *Rabelais* 240–41).[19] Women's gaping "rien-à-voir" functions as a potentially castrating *vagina dentata*. This is just one cultural instance of the fear that women—specifically female morphology—supposedly inspire in men.

McCullers's fictional worlds are worlds "between men" or "homosocial," to use Sedgwick's term that describes "the spectrum of male bonds that includes but is not limited to the 'homosexual'" (*Between Men* 85). Sedgwick argues that in the male domain, women function as barter-objects so that men might "touch" *each other*. In the seemingly heterosexual romantic triangle, it is the *other man* who is the true goal of the male lover.[20] This observation provides a key to the "open secret" of the all-male desire hinted at in *The Ballad of the Sad Café*. Although Marvin Macy and Cousin Lymon are not, strictly speaking, rivals for the hand of Miss Amelia, they nevertheless use her so that they might gain access to each other—Lymon for love, Marvin to avenge Miss Amelia through jealousy.

Penderton, Leonora, and Major Langdon form another sort of erotic triangle. Leonora and the Major are having an extramarital affair while Penderton, who "had a sad penchant for becoming enamoured of his wife's lovers" (*R* 15), rather than protesting against his cuckolding, comes "to feel an emotional regard for the Major that was the nearest thing to love that he had ever known" (*R* 33). Sedgwick reads cuckolding as "a sexual act, performed on a man, by another man," which means, then, that "heterosexual love . . . [is] a strategy of homosexual desire" (*Between Men* 49). Although Sedgwick's conclusion is bold, it does mirror McCullers's narrative: Penderton "was just as jealous of his wife as he was of her love" (*R* 33); Leonora is the "gift" Penderton offers to both his own and her potential lovers. On the whole, however, male-male desire in McCullers's fiction does not need women as conduits, for the simple reason that, as I have already noted, women are strikingly and frequently absent from the workings of desire. In place of heterosexual desire is the homosocial, embodied in the chain gang, the café, and, most notably, the army. Rarely is there a female equivalent to such male space in McCullers's writings.[21]

The image of the chain gang in the coda of *The Ballad of the Sad Café*, "The Twelve Mortal Men," might embody the homosocial.[22] The men, both black and white, "who are together," are "chained at the ankles" (84). While the coda might show "how men can achieve creativity . . . even in the most difficult situations if there is harmony and cooperation" (Millichap, "Carson McCullers" 338), the following examples suggest that the chain gang itself is certainly a very compact location of all-male relations, intensified by the chains that yoke the men together.[23]

Another all-male location is the café, the focus of *The Ballad of the Sad Café, The Heart Is a Lonely Hunter,* and "A Tree, A Rock, A Cloud." The only women who have anything to do with cafés are the mannish Miss Amelia, the tomboy adolescents, Mick Kelly and Frankie Addams, and Alice Brannon, wife of a café owner. Amelia is punished for overstepping the mark,[24] Alice dies, and Frankie Addams's visit to the Blue Moon ends in her attempted rape. These examples effectively point to the antagonism shown toward women in a male zone. The café, like the world of the racetrack of "The Jockey" and the agora of ancient Athens, is a meeting place for the free male citizen.

Biff Brannon, owner of the New York Café, dreams of ancient Greece, of "[w]alking in sandals on the edge of the blue Aegean. The loose robes girdled at the waist. Children. The marble baths and the contemplations in the temples" (*H* 201). The reference to children here may recall the ancient practice of pederasty, or "Greek love."[25] Ancient Greece conjures up a homosocial world, exclusive of women who were classed with children, slaves, and foreigners, that is, as other. Furthermore, images of the classical world offer "models of virilizing male bonds, models in which the male homosocial institutions (education, political mentorship, brotherhood in arms) and the homosexual seemed to be fully continuous, and fully exclude the world of women" (Sedgwick, *Between Men* 207).[26]

Just as Biff yearns for the male world of ancient Greece, Captain Penderton, in *Reflections in a Golden Eye*, reveals a "predilection" for the Middle Ages. Society in the Middle Ages was strongly homosocial, as exemplified by the prevalence and power of monastic institutions and such groups as the Knights Templar, rumored to have practiced sodomy. And so Penderton's "imaginings of the barracks were flavored by this medievalist predilection." Accordingly, he envies the life of Private Williams and the other enlisted men, "eating and laughing together with lusty camaraderie" (95).

As Penderton's obsession with Williams mounts, he begins to wish that he were merely an enlisted man, "'Private Weldon Penderton.' And these words, with the associations they engendered, aroused in the Captain a perverse feeling of relief and satisfaction" (109). Several cultural historians have remarked on the binding force of homosexual desire in institutions like the army,[27] and this helps bring to light the eroticization of male-male relations in *Reflections in a Golden Eye*.[28] Captain Penderton yearns for "the hubbub of young male voices, the genial loafing in the sun, the irresponsible shenanigans of camaraderie" (109), and "[w]ith deep secret longing he thought of the barracks, seeing in his mind the neat cots placed in a row, the bare floors, and stark curtainless windows."[29] Depicted as "austere and ascetic" (117), the army life in McCullers's fiction is manifestly homosocial.

The disciplinary measures and normative aims typical of military life structure the army in *Reflections in a Golden Eye* but in an unusual way: removed from the feminizing, and thus supposedly enervating, influences of female contact, it produces virility through the association of males with males.[30] Accordingly, Major Langdon tells Penderton that he wishes Anacleto, the Langdons' eunuch-like Filipino houseboy, would join the army since "'it might have made a man of him'" (112). In light of the current argument and of the comment that follows ("'it is better . . . for the square peg to keep scraping around the round hole than to discover and use the unorthodox hole that would fit it'"), the irony of Langdon's remark should not be overlooked. For, in *Reflections in a Golden Eye*, the army does "make men of" its recruits, yet in a rather different manner from that imagined by Langdon. The army is, rather, a potential site of seething same-sex passion.[31]

The irony of several of McCullers's readers' comments is similarly revealing. For example, Oliver Evans believes that in *The Heart Is a Lonely Hunter*, "[t]he wish to love . . . tends to join men together, often without their realizing it" ("Case of the Silent Singer" 199). Most commentators have similarly and surprisingly overlooked the homosocial (which includes the homo*sexual*) tension in McCullers's portrayal of the army. Rather, they claim, McCullers chose the army for the story's setting only to accentuate the monotony and conformity that often define her southern towns.[32] These are, of course, pertinent descriptions of the army post, but they fail to take into account the strong erotic overtones of "men who are together." While the chain gang, the café, and the army in McCullers's texts are all images of brotherhood, it is the army in particular that produces the all-masculine, virile body, that classic body so utterly opposed to the feminized grotesque body.

Thus far, then, I have suggested that McCullers portrays the homosocial and the concomitant rejection of heterosexuality as an anxious and disgusted reaction to grotesque womanliness. While the female body is grotesque, the ideal virile body is analogous to the classic body, an "impenetrable façade" (Bakhtin, *Rabelais* 29). According to this corporeal schema, a woman's body is fluid while a man's is hard; fleshy while his is taut; penetrable while he (the penetrator) is impenetrable. It is this virile body that is often central to McCullers's presentation of the homoerotic couple because male same-sex desire has a virilizing force; it is as if manliness rubs off on the lover and/or the beloved.

One example of the virile body in McCullers's writings is the all-too-masculine Marvin Macy in *The Ballad of the Sad Café*.[33] Marvin Macy is a rough, tough he-man who has "degraded and shamed" many of the town's virgins. He is "the handsomest man in this region—being six feet one inch tall, hard-muscled. . . . He was an evil character . . . [and] carried about with him the dried and salted ear of a man he had killed in a razor fight" (34–35). Marvin Macy's performance of phallic virility eventually earns the admiration of the effeminate Lymon, who is "tantalized" (53) by this exotic stranger.[34] Marvin Macy is what we might today call a "stud": the "real" man, virile and masculine.[35]

Virility takes another form in *Reflections in a Golden Eye*. Private Williams, the beautiful boy of nature, a Gauguin-like primitif, is perfect in "the pure-cut lines of the young man's body" (74). Williams's predecessor is Melville's Billy Budd, who has "as much of masculine beauty as one can expect anywhere to see." Melville compares Billy, in turn, with a Greek sculpture of the "heroic strong man, Hercules" and with a "young Achilles" (331, 329, 349). Similarly, D. H. Lawrence's "well-built" orderly in "The Prussian Officer" is another example of pagan beauty: "He had strong, heavy limbs. . . . There was something altogether warm and young about him" (9).

McCullers's portrayal of Private Williams clearly echoes those of Lawrence's orderly and Melville's Billy Budd. As the orderly is "like a wild thing" (Lawrence 9), so, too, is Williams "a wild creature" (*R* 8) who "held himself erect. Without his clothes he was so slim that the pure, curved lines of his ribs could be seen" (*R* 56). Penderton is overwhelmed by "the fine, skilful hands and the tender roundness of [his] neck" (*R* 77), just as the Prussian Officer marks "the bend of [the orderly's] neck" and his "young, brown, shapely peasant's hands" (Lawrence 9).

McCullers alludes to the self-containment of the coldly beautiful Williams over and over again throughout *Reflections in a Golden Eye*. He is often "silent" with "the mute expression of animals" (8), and he displays no emotion: "[H]e had [never] been known to laugh, to become angry, [nor] to suffer in any way" (8). Like Lawrence's orderly and Melville's Billy Budd, Williams recalls the classic male body the ancient Greeks and the Renaissance so admired, exemplified in Michelangelo's David. This ephebic body is next to godliness, an Apolline gesture toward pure untrammeled beauty. Opposed to this is the female body, "the soft luxurious warmth of woman-flesh, the quiet darkness" (*R* 123) that is a fearful contaminant.

Like Williams, Singer is silent: he is a deaf-mute. *The Heart Is a Lonely Hunter* reinforces the portrait of Singer as an inviolable male subject: he is described as "inscrutable" (86). In her outline of "The Mute," McCullers writes that "nothing that goes on around [Singer] disturbs his inner self," so "no attempt will be made to enter intimately into his subconscious" ("Author's Outline" 138). Neither readers nor Singer's fellow characters can violate him. He shores himself up, refuses to open. Accordingly, Singer is "erect and tense" (*H* 189): he "stood very straight with his hands in his pockets" (*H* 8). As such, he resembles the jockey, Bitsy Barlow ("Jockey" 103), and Captain Penderton. Barlow's "body is as hard as a lead soldier's" ("Jockey" 108), and the Captain is "stiff" (*R* 12, 118), "very straight" (*R* 22), and "tense" (*R* 67, 107). With a "hard mouth"

(*R* 77), he is "rigid and unemotional" (*R* 94). The virile body, it seems, is an erect *phallic* body. It is this body which is adored and produced in the homosocial space of male-male desire and which is firmly opposed to the messy female body branded as a grotesque gaping wound, threatening castration. The high erotic value put on both masculinity and male-male relations in McCullers's texts arises in response to "the terrible sickness of women." Man is in "flight from woman."

GROTESQUE PLEASURES

There is little doubt that the celebration of maleness occurs to a large extent at the expense of femaleness in McCullers's writings. But to claim that male homosexuality comes about solely as a disgusted response to women recalls the "logic" that a woman only becomes a lesbian as a result of previous bad experiences with men. There is one fault line in the celebration of ideal classic masculinity, however, and this lies in the ironic association of the virile body with the male *hysterical* body. Psychoanalytic theory holds that male hysteria is a response to the fearful, castrating, grotesque woman. Hysteria in the male, first of all, implies a feminization from which he is supposedly fleeing. Second, the association of ideal manhood with hysteria suggests that virility itself is a sickness, thus undermining its exemplary status. Third, and more important, the homoerotic body opposes itself to cultural norms through its seeking of nonfunctionary bodily pleasures. An exploration of male hysteria and (auto-)erotic pleasures will illustrate the *excess* of the homoerotic body and its close alignment with the grotesque.

"Phallic panic," the term Barbara Creed uses to describe male hysteria, is "a defense against the possibility of *symbolic castration*," symbolic because it can refer to any separation the infant experiences as "a loss of something which it feels is an integral part of its own body—such as separation from the womb or the loss of the mother's breast" (129). Creed also claims that male hysteria emerges as a result of fear of the grotesque female body, which threatens to engulf the male subject. To allay his castration anxiety, the male hysteric seeks to duplicate himself, to find a reflection of himself in an other to confirm the presence of the penis. In the male homosexual relationship, the lover is assured of possession of the penis, represented by either a like phallic (male) other or by his own phallicized body. His fears of the castrating woman are thus assuaged. For, as Freud suggests, "to display the penis (or any of its surrogates) is to say: 'I am not afraid of you. I defy you. I have a penis'" ("Medusa's Head" 274).

McCullers's texts frequently represent the phallicization of the whole body of the lover himself and/or the beloved in this way. As I have already suggested, Penderton, Williams, Singer, and Bitsy Barlow are, like Lawrence's Prussian Officer, rigid and inviolable—in a word, virile.[36] Under this rubric, it becomes increasingly clear how we can equiparate the idealized virile body and the hysterical male body. It is as if the whole virile body is paralyzed in a form of priapic rigor mortis, "stiff with terror" at the moment of its very phallicization. To claim that the exemplary male virile body is also the *hysterical* male body is to undermine and question the very standard against which woman is defined as grotesque. For it appears that the standard—the idealized classic male body—might be as excessive and as grotesque as its female counterpart. In this way, categories of normal and abnormal identities no longer make sense.

The stiffness and rigidity of virility is also a symptom of male hysteria in terms of impotent paralysis: "[h]is organ is struck dumb" (Creed 132).[37] McCullers similarly casts the homosexual lover as the impotent hysteric in her "almost gay" novels: Penderton's homosexuality "is . . . a symbol . . . of impotence" ("Flowering Dream" 282).[38] Impotence, a result of phallic panic, is a symbol or expression of both hysteria[39] and homosexuality in McCullers's texts because, confronted with woman, Penderton's organ is paralyzed. He is compared to a broken doll (*R* 72) and a broken monk (*R* 125), both powerful images of impotence.

Furthermore, "[s]exually the Captain obtained within himself a delicate balance between the male and female elements, with the susceptibilities of both the sexes and the active powers of none" (*R* 4). Thus, when Leonora "married the Captain she had been a virgin. Four nights after her wedding she was still a virgin, and in the fifth night her status was changed only enough to leave her somewhat puzzled. As for the rest it would be hard to say" (*R* 20). Penderton's impotence is once more suggested through Leonora's jibe about his poor "horsemanship," which greatly "piques" the Captain (*R* 115).

In *The Heart Is a Lonely Hunter,* Biff Brannon is also impotent; this is the "special physical part kept always guarded" (29). The figure of Biff provides an interesting example of "perverse" desire because he does not fall into the category of the same-sex passion I outlined above. Nevertheless, his impotence does arise from phallic panic, manifested as the flight from woman. Thinking back to his sexual heyday, Biff recalls when "he suddenly lost it. When he could lie with a woman no longer" (208). And so Biff and Alice sleep in shifts, and he will not undress in front of her. Biff tells his sister-in-law, Lucile, that he is no longer interested in "any kind of throbs either way" (117). This is not quite true, for he entertains a strange desire for the adolescent tomboy Mick Kelly. However, once Mick reaches puberty and becomes a "woman," Biff's desire is dampened. She, like Alice, now bears the potential for castration.

The literary substitution of paralysis of the organ—impotence—for a displaced homosexuality[40] draws on the negative cultural association of homosexuality with infertility, unproductiveness, and, ultimately, death. Within this framework, homosexuality is abnormal, since it denies or negates the function of human sexuality: procreation. This threatens the conservation of social relations for which reproduction of the species and labor is a vital and necessary achievement. As Biff Brannon succinctly words it, "Life was only a matter of intake and alimentation and reproduction" (*H* 204). While I have suggested that all subjectivity can be construed as grotesque in her texts, McCullers simultaneously, and rather disquietingly, deploys rather orthodox images of homosexual men in terms of both homosexual flight from woman and impotence.

However, a closer look at McCullers's portrayals of homosexual men and desire reveals that she is struggling to override such dangerous stereotyping. More promisingly, her texts show a radical turn toward exploring other modes of living and desiring that lie beyond the realms of convention and moral judgment. I want to show that the phallic panic of the homosexual characters in McCullers's texts creates new bodily pleasures and so produces new modes of relationship between men, and between men and the world.

As Freud argues, homosexuality (for him, one of the perversions) challenges "the normal sexual aim," that is, "the union of the genitals in the act known as copulation." Instead, "[p]erversions are sexual activities which either (a) extend, in an anatomical sense, beyond the regions of the body that are designed for sexual union, or (b) linger over the intermediate relations to the sexual object which should normally be traversed rapidly on the path towards the final sexual aim" ("Sexual Aberrations" 62). In contrast to reproductive heterosexuality then, homosexual desire "puts the body and the world of objects to uses that have nothing whatever to do with any kind of 'immanent' design or purpose" (Silverman 187). We see this dynamic in McCullers's writings in the *vicarious* nature of male-male desire, most notably in Captain Penderton's ecstatic ride on the stallion, Firebird. A tempestuous animal who moves with "fiery grace" (*R* 25), Firebird is a Lawrentian symbol of sensuousness and a substitute for more orthodox channels of desire for Penderton. The Captain's experience with the stallion has the effect of orgasm, of sexual excitement and satisfaction, providing him with a powerful expression of vicarious desire as well as confirmation and enjoyment of the penis/phallus. In true carnivalesque style, then, the worlds of the human and the animal become confused.

In *The Heart Is a Lonely Hunter,* the vicarious nature of "other" desires occurs in a nightmare[41] in which Antonapoulos offers a phallic image to Singer. Singer dreams that Antonapoulos kneels naked at the top of a stone staircase, "and fumbled with something that he held above his head and gazed at it as though in prayer. He himself knelt half-way down the steps. He was naked and cold and he could not take his eyes from Antonapoulos and the thing he held above him. . . . He awoke with a jerk" (192). The text does not make clear exactly what the "thing" is that Antonapoulos holds above his head as an object of worship. It has been suggested that it is a Christian cross; further on in the story, when Singer visits the asylum, he watches as Antonapoulos "fumbled for something in his bosom. It was the little brass cross that he had always worn. . . . Singer thought of the dream" (196).[42] The "thing" of the dream is perhaps "a religious offering being proffered to some person or object" (Dodd 207).[43] This is consistent with a common reading of *The Heart Is a Lonely Hunter* that posits Singer as some form of deity, a God or Christ figure.[44] However, more germane to this discussion is to read the "thing" as a penis, as Emily Budick does. Budick recalls that "one of the few ways in which Antonapoulos uses his hands is to . . . indulge in his 'solitary pleasure,' masturbation" (148).[45] The association with the penis here suggests that

Antonapoulos provides Singer with the penis-phallus; he fulfills the role of the unnamed "thing." It is enough for Singer to wake "with a jerk."

Vicarious and thus perverse desire also comes to the fore in the fetishization of hands, ubiquitous in *The Heart Is a Lonely Hunter* and prominent as well in *Reflections in a Golden Eye.* For example, Captain Penderton, like Antonapoulos (*H* 194), has "white, fattish hands" and wears a ring (*R* 10). In contrast, Private Williams's hands are "small, delicately boned, and very strong" (*R* 8).[46] The thought of these hands makes Penderton shiver (*R* 98). In *The Heart Is a Lonely Hunter,* Biff Brannon is often described mashing his nose with his fingers. Frances Paden reads this as a symbol of masturbation. (Again, the text's portrayal of the nonhomosexual Biff unsettles any neat presumptions as to what characterizes homosexuality.) Although there of course need be no necessary connection between masturbation and same-sex desire, masturbation does have something in common with homosexual desire: both are "unnatural" because they defy reproductive sexuality. Furthermore, masturbation involves the eroticization of one's *own* body and thus might be construed a homosexual act. This is why Mick Kelly's younger brother, Bubber, must stop this perverse practice if he is to grow up to be a "man," to become "George" (*H* 151). It is the trope of the hands that is tied up with forbidden desire, masturbatory or homosexual.

Although not mentioned in any of McCullers's essays, Anderson's *Winesburg, Ohio* lingers in the background of McCullers's grotesque worlds.[47] Most pertinent here is Anderson's tale "Hands," exemplifying the use of hands as the site of unnatural desire and shedding light on the powerful motif of Singer's hands in *The Heart Is a Lonely Hunter.* In Anderson's story, Wing Biddlebaum is known for his "slender expressive fingers, forever active, forever striving to conceal themselves," which are likened to "the beating of the wings of an imprisoned bird." Biddlebaum's "nervous little hands" become an expression of the homoerotic: in "their feeling for the boys under their charge such men are not unlike the finer sort of women in their love of men." Biddlebaum dreams of "a kind of pastoral golden age. Across a green open country came clean-limbed young men. . . . In crowds the young men came to gather about the feet of an old man" (30).[48] Biddlebaum's days as a schoolteacher end with "the tragedy": one of the young boys, "enamoured" of his teacher, dreams "unspeakable things" of Biddlebaum and "in the morning went forth to tell his dreams as facts." Driven out of town, Biddlebaum now goes about "striving to conceal his hands," for "[a]gain and again the fathers of the boys had talked of the hands. 'Keep your hands to yourself'" (27–33). The hands, then, become a symbol of a forbidden homoerotic desire.

Of course, hands come to the fore in *The Heart Is a Lonely Hunter* through Singer's signing. McCullers's descriptions of his hands immediately recall Biddlebaum's hands: nervous and fidgety, with attempts at their concealment. Alone once Antonapoulos is admitted to the asylum, Singer walks with his "hands stuffed tight in the pockets of his trousers" (15). He has no use for them: he has nothing to say, no one to say it to. Yet, his hands take on a life of their own: "His hands were a torment to him. They would not rest. They twitched in his sleep, and sometimes he awoke to find them shaping the words in his dreams before his face. . . . [S]ometimes when he was alone and his thoughts were with [Antonapoulos] his hands would begin to shape the words before he knew it. Then when he realized he was like a man caught talking aloud to himself. . . . The shame and the sorrow mixed together and he doubled his hands and put them behind him. But they would not let him rest" (182). The activity of Singer's hands causes him *shame*, just as Antonapoulos's hands in the dream cause him to wake in fear. As Budick comments, "Singer might well feel afraid of what he has witnessed in his dream of raw and naked desire. He may have very good reasons for refusing to say what thing he has seen" (148).[49] Any form of autoeroticism must menace the aim of "natural love": the survival of the species through procreation.

The shame Singer experiences occurs once more. Singer, "[a]lthough he had been deaf since he was an infant, . . . had not always been a real mute."[50] Sent to an institution for the deaf, Singer learned to sign, and "finally he had been taught to speak. . . . It was not natural to him, and his tongue felt like a whale in his mouth. . . . He felt that there was something disgusting in his speech. . . . When he was twenty-two . . . he had met Antonapoulos. . . . Since that time he had never spoken with his mouth again" (14). The mention of the whale might recall Melville's Moby Dick, that legendary phallic symbol. While this passage could suggest a "withdrawal from sexual relations" (Budick 151), the sexual nature of the image may indicate that Singer's whale-tongue is a phallus substitute. It fills his mouth and prevents him from speaking; it is a strange autoerotic oral desire that "disgusts" Singer.

A second example of the eroticization of body parts other than the more sexually conventional ones in McCullers's novels is the eye. In "The Sexual Aberrations," Freud claims that since looking is derived from touching, it is a frequent catalyst for sexual stimulation and excitement. Importantly, scopophilia only "becomes a perversion . . . if, [among other things] instead of being *preparatory* to the normal sexual aim, it supplants it" (69–70). It is such scopophilia in which Captain Penderton engages.[51] While Williams looks blankly past Captain Penderton (*R* 94), the Captain constantly watches Williams (*R* 73–74, 77, 92, 94, 109, 119), causing "his throat to contract so that he could not swallow" (*R* 94). (Is this another example of the whale-tongue?) The eye becomes an erotogenic zone again when, during his frenzied ride on Firebird, Penderton has a vision: "His eyes were glassy and half-open, as in delirium . . . each of the multiple visions which he saw impressed itself on his mind with burning vividness" (*R* 70). The eye has become the site of "burning" orgasmic pleasure.

Imagery to do with eyes and looking also dominates the trope of narcissism, which to some extent also structures homosexuality in McCullers's texts. Narcissism is dangerously implicit in cultural perceptions of homosexual passion, encouraged by Freud,[52] which stress the sameness of the lover and the love-object. That "homo" is Greek for "the same" enhances this belief that homosexuality involves a reflection of the same, where difference is not *apparent*. Homosexuality is not visible as is, for instance, race and gender (Sedgwick, *Epistemology* 75).[53] This reinforces the common misconception that homosexuality pivots on an economy of the same and is thus "sterile." The sterility invoked by the image of the doll, to which Penderton is likened, is reinforced by the fact that the doll is at one time *reflected* in his soul (*R* 113).

The question of homosexuality's extremely problematic association with narcissism[54] perfectly highlights McCullers's ambitious and admirable struggle to depict grotesque alternative desires and behaviors without collapsing into stereotypical and therefore damaging imagery and language. On the one hand, McCullers stresses the *differences* between each member of the homosexual couple. Accordingly, *The Heart Is a Lonely*

Hunter opens with: "The two friends [Singer and Antonapoulos] were very different" (7). Penderton and Williams are also markedly different, as will become clear later in this chapter. On the other hand, both *The Heart Is a Lonely Hunter* and *Reflections in a Golden Eye* participate in representations of homosexuality in terms of narcissism.

Narcissism rests on mirroring images, where the self is reflected back via an intermediary, as with the doll that is copied onto Penderton's soul. Such imagery persists in both novels. For example, every payday Antonapoulos has his photograph taken (*H* 9). More significantly, in Antonapoulos's eyes, Singer "saw the little rectangled pictures of himself that he had watched a thousand times" (*H* 194).[55] That Singer uses Antonapoulos as his mirror, as a blank canvas, is enhanced by the fact that Singer both writes and busily signs to Antonapoulos although he knows that the latter can neither read nor understand sign language. "But it did not matter" (*H* 8).

Self-reflection is also at work in *Reflections in a Golden Eye,* where eyes do not see, they merely reflect. For example, just as the Captain is about to mount Firebird, he "looked into the horse's round, purple eyes and saw there a liquid image of his own frightened face" (67). Penderton's own eyes are portrayed as "glassy" (10, 70). Similarly reflective, the eyes of the Private are "mute" (8) and unseeing (94, 120). He only *watches* during those evenings spent gazing voyeuristically at Leonora Penderton, who "[i]n him was a deep reflection" (29).

There is one occasion, however, during which Captain Penderton really "sees." Again, it is during his ecstatic horse ride. Having achieved an orgasmic state, he has a "kaleidoscopic" vision. Besides its scopophilic intention, "the multiple visions" experienced by Penderton suggest an otherness outside of flat two-way reflection. Something more is happening here. The aforementioned "liquid" image, along with the "distorted" image Penderton sees reflected in his soul (*R* 113), also suggests a kaleidoscopic fluidity and excess, beyond stagnant self-identity. In this way, narcissism appears not as a state of reflective closure but as a *dynamic*—of movement and thus of possible transformation. Thus, while in Ovid's original tale of Narcissus the pond reflects the beautiful and virile Apollonian boy, in *Reflections in a Golden Eye* the way in which reflection is distorted suggests the grotesque. Anacleto, watching one of his paintings burn in the fireplace, likens it to "'[a] peacock of a sort of ghastly green. With one immense golden eye. And in it these reflections of something tiny and—' . . . 'Grotesque,' [Alison] finished for him" (*R* 87). *Grotesque* reflection, then, may indicate an excessive form of subjectivity.

I want to suggest then that McCullers's portrayal of homosexuality's ostensible dependence on sameness demands that we rethink the very structure of narcissism—as a form of self-transformation that creates new forms of subjectivity, in terms of the play between self and other. This idea of metamorphosis occurs in two quite different incidents. On Antonapoulos's death, Singer takes on his dead friend's qualities: he makes "a great to-do" when his coin gets stuck in a slot machine, and he steals soap and other items from the hotel room (*H* 284).[56] Singer becomes *another*, thus exceeding the bounds of an enclosed, simply narcissistic subjectivity. In a similar way, Penderton seeks to become the other-beloved. He daydreams of becoming a private like Williams, "a twin almost of the soldier he hated—with a young, easy body . . . , with thick glossy hair and round eyes unshadowed" (*R* 109).

Thus, the flat mirror—the glassy and blind eyes in *Reflections in a Golden Eye* and the photographs and endless reflection in *The Heart Is a Lonely Hunter*—cannot represent the multiplicity of the body's pleasures. The type of subjectivity that McCullers creates is not a subjectivity open to representation in a flat mirror. Rather, it is the grotesque subject who might signal perverse desire: the reflections in Penderton's own soul, in the eye of the stallion, and in the eye of the "ghastly" peacock produce the distorted or "liquid" image. These images anticipate Frankie Addams's contorted reflection in the watery kitchen mirror in *The Member of the Wedding* (8), which promises a becoming-other. The distortion of grotesque reflection in *Reflections in a Golden Eye* is not the objective mirror of art (Evans, *Carson McCullers* 71); it comes closer to the speculum, Luce Irigaray's curved, anamorphic mirror, which implies an excessive, deviant sexuality and the creation of new selves.

The forms of alternative pleasure enjoyed and produced by the homoerotic body similarly offer transformative promise. Thus, like narcissism, autoeroticism takes the body as both subject and object, as both producer and receiver of pleasure. Although nonheterosexual desires may be, strictly speaking, unprocreative, such bodily pleasures invent other subjectivities. As Jacques Derrida notes of autoeroticism, "one . . . makes oneself other by oneself" because "[w]hat is touching is touched" (153–54). In creating metamorphic relations between the self and its other self (or selves), and between the self and an other, the homoerotic body of McCullers's texts swells beyond its limits in a shattering of the self.

This movement is also apparent in sadism and masochism, in which the male lovers of *Reflections in a Golden Eye* and *The Heart Is a Lonely Hunter* indulge. For Freud, both the sadist and the masochist ignore the "normal" sexual aim ("Sexual Aberrations" 71–73).[57] Masochistic traits appear in both Singer and Penderton; Singer's suicide is the ultimate act of masochism. Although the masochist substitutes pain for pleasure, thus creating a new shape of desire, he or she risks self-enclosure—a risk also inherent in narcissism—and what follows is the death of the subject, as literally represented in Singer's death.

Captain Penderton also indulges in masochism: "In his balance between the two great instincts, towards life and towards death, the scale was heavily weighted to one side—to death" (*R* 15). Thus, as a boy, he gave a "love offering" to "the school-yard bully who had once beaten him" (*R* 51), reflecting the narrator's claim in *The Ballad of the Sad Café* that the "lover craves any possible relation with the beloved, even if this experience can cause him only pain" (34). And the Captain hates riding: "[H]e only rode because it was the thing to do, and because this was another one of his ways of tormenting himself" (*R* 68). He chooses a "clumsy" army saddle instead of his wife's more comfortable one (*R* 68). As he (sadistically) gives Firebird rein and then draws him in again, Penderton derives a parallel masochistic pleasure from his "strange and secret little penances" (*R* 68).[58]

However, like narcissism, masochism might also enact self-metamorphosis. Kaja Silverman calls the bodily excess of masochism "ecstatic delirium," for one is "*beside oneself*" (263, emphasis added). This "ex-stasy" occurs in Penderton's ride on Firebird, whom he associates with Private Williams (*R* 14). It is an epiphanic moment for the Captain, an almost out-of-body experience.[59] As the stallion tears wildly through the forest, Penderton, barely able to whisper "'I am lost,'" gives "up life [and] suddenly began to live. A great mad joy surged through him" (*R* 70). The kaleidoscopic vision he experiences causes him to feel as if "he had soared to the rare level of consciousness where the mystic feels that the earth is he and that he is the earth. There was a grin of bloody rapture on his mouth" (*R* 70–71). Penderton is *beside himself*, as he experiences a "little death," a grotesque blurring of self and world. Masochistic ecstasy moves toward the creation of a new self mixed in with the world, invoking Frankie Addams's "we of me" fantasy.

When Penderton finally dismounts after the terrifying ride, he "broke off a long switch, and with the last of his spent strength he began to beat the horse savagely. . . . The Captain kept on beating him. Then at last the horse stood motionless and gave a broken sigh" (*R* 71). Firebird is "soaked with sweat and there were welts on his rump. In one afternoon the horse seemed to have changed from a thoroughbred to a plug fit for the plough" (*R* 73). Penderton's sadism is alluded to throughout the text, for example, in his cruel treatment of a kitten (*R* 16) and of Alison Langdon, whom "[f]requently, in many mean and subtle ways, the Captain tried to hurt" (*R* 34).[60] The Captain needs someone to hate (*R* 50) and "this hatred [is as] passionate as love" (*R* 74). Penderton's changing attitude toward Williams further reveals his sadistic tendencies. Moving beyond his initial annoyance and then hatred (*R* 108), Penderton "was conscious only of the irresistible yearning to break down the barrier between them. When from a distance he saw the soldier, . . . he wanted to shout to him, or to strike him with his fist, to make him respond in some way to violence" (*R* 118). Here, sadism would seem to offer—or at least suggest the desire for—the repudiation of otherness. Silverman describes this desire as the subsumption of an other by the self. Like narcissism and masochism, then, sadism is an expansion of the "I," but this time through the inhabitation of another by the self (270–86).

In *The Heart Is a Lonely Hunter*, "self-extension" occurs in a nonviolent manner. Singer, like Penderton, also yearns to "break down the barrier" between himself and Antonapoulos but in a rather mystical way. On the train to visit Antonapoulos in the asylum, Singer looks out at the passing countryside and notes that "[t]his kaleidoscopic variety of scene . . . seemed somehow connected with his friend. His thoughts were with Antonapoulos. The bliss of their reunion almost stifled him" (282).

As he thinks back over the past half-year of their separation, he acknowledges that "[b]ehind each waking moment there had always been his friend. And this submerged communion with Antonapoulos had grown and changed as if they were together in the flesh" (282). And in Singer's dreams "they were always together" (177). These visions of communion are made flesh, so to speak, in Singer's narcissistic appropriation of Antonapoulos's characteristics, which I noted earlier.

Singer's suicide—significantly, with the phallus-pistol, suggesting once more a "petite mort"—after the death of Antonapoulos is the ultimate attempt to break through a numb otherness. Singer and Antonapoulos can only be "as one" in death. Just as *The Heart Is a Lonely Hunter* ends with the motif of masochistic violence, so too the sadism of *Reflections in a Golden Eye* culminates in Penderton's shooting of Williams, an act of "revenge for the beloved's betrayal" (Adams 63), but also an act of penetration. The murder (again with a pistol) also violates the boundary between self and other. Both actions are the result of "the irresistible yearning to break down the barrier" between self and other. Perhaps it is only in death that the ultimate goal of sadomasochistic violence can be achieved: "For the dead can claim / The lover's senses, the mortgaged heart" (*Mortgaged Heart* 165).

Thus, while McCullers ostensibly draws on traditional tropes to portray nonheterosexual desire in her novels, such as sterility, autoeroticism, narcissism, and sadism and masochism, she does so in a way that forces us to rethink the very nature of these dynamics. In this sense, her depiction of homosexuality is a complex one, no less so for the fact that it is hard to pin down the act itself in any of her texts. What she is doing, however, is attempting to portray "odd" desire outside of claustrophobic stereotypes. The type of desire she describes is troubling not because it is "unnatural" and unprocreative but because it is expansive, shattering, and thus truly and radically grotesque.

Finally, McCullers makes use of the binary masculine/feminine and the associated binaries of sanity/insanity, innocence/decadence, and so forth in her portrayal of homosexual desire. However, in using these burdensome structural features of homosexuality that so often remain unchallenged, she at the same time undermines them, forcing us to renegotiate the treacherous realms of desire.

FEMINIZATION OF THE VIRILE BODY

If the human body and its discursive representations are analogous to the workings and conceptions of the social body, it follows that homoerotic desire, which, as I have shown, overflows the bounds of the ideal and discrete subject, is thus a polluting threat to the fiction of heterosexual social harmony. In the America of McCullers's time, homosexuals, ostracized as some kind of defiling force, faced the real risk of social punishment: harassment and arrest, for example. And throughout the ages, homosexuality has been treated as both a mental and a physical illness or pollutant, just as in *The Heart Is a Lonely Hunter* Antonapoulos is put out of contaminating reach in the mental asylum. Perhaps not surprisingly then, in 1952, the American Psychiatric Association formally classified homosexuality as an illness (Abelove 67).

McCullers's portrayal of Captain Penderton's perverse obsession similarly stresses pathological symptoms. Throughout *Reflections in a Golden Eye* he is constantly "agitated" (12)[61] by the young Private Williams: he experiences an "aching want" (93);[62] he feels "dizzy" to think of the young man (93); and he "shivers" (98) and becomes disoriented at the sight of Williams so that he "suffered a curious lapse of sensory impressions; . . . he found himself unable to see or hear properly" (93) or swallow (94). Consequently, Penderton feels a victim of a witch's charm for he "was in a state of sharpened sensitivity close to delirium" (117). Furthermore, he rapidly ages, develops a tic in his eye (107), and loses his powers of speech in the midst of delivering a lecture (118).

Reflections in a Golden Eye depicts homosexuality not only as mental illness but also as *physical* illness. Accordingly, Penderton's desire for Williams "grew in him like a disease," like the cancerous cells that "rebel and begin the insidious self-multiplications that will ultimately destroy the body" (108). For today's readers especially, in the context of the AIDS pandemic, this is a dominant cultural metaphor of homosexual passion: it is a disease, in need of curing. Not only would homosexuality threaten the survival of the species with its "sterility," but it would also seem to have the power to contaminate the individual practitioner himself, in the same way that Captain Penderton's *own* desire affects him so adversely.

In *Reflections in a Golden Eye*, the homosexual lover also infects the beloved, just as femininity and womanhood seem to contaminate masculinity. The Penderton-Williams relationship develops the trope of a polluting homosexuality in the oppositions nature/culture or civilization and innocence/corruption.[63] The homosexual male is, according to stereotype, the urbane corrupter of an innocent pastoral of youth. Many of McCullers's commentators have argued for this seemingly easy division of the homosexual Captain Penderton and the object of his passion, the primitive Elgee Williams, into the categories of "culture/civilization" and "nature," respectively, whereby the former is inferior to the latter.[64] The beloved is the pure boy of nature who is ruined by the urbane officer. According to this reading, Captain Penderton is the uptight civilized man of culture. "[A] great swell," he is "a connoisseur of good food and a neat amateur chef" (*R* 111), a man of some intellect and "something of a savant. . . . His head was filled with statistics and information of scholarly exactitude" (*R* 15). Penderton also has a strong impulse toward death (*R* 15),[65] which opposes him to life. Consequently, he either fears the natural world[66] or perverts it.[67]

In supposed contrast, the twenty-year-old Private Williams is a dumb innocent (*R* 8) who is unreflective, acting only on instinct. Only four times has Williams ever acted on his own accord and even then he does not know why (*R* 30).[68] Unlike Penderton, who is associated with lifelessness, Williams is constantly associated with the natural world: the sun (*R* 8, 56), the forest (*R* 8, 56), and animals (*R* 8, 25, 30). "A wild creature" (*R* 8), he has a "mute" animal-like expression (*R* 8, 94, 120) with a "sensual, savage smile" (*R* 56).

Again, McCullers seems to be deploying orthodox imagery to describe homosexual desire, the homosexual lover and his love-object. However, McCullers in fact distorts this simple characterization of Williams, which assumes that the natural is good. Williams's "naturalness" is as perverse and twisted as Penderton's "culture." For example, Williams kills a man over a mere wheelbarrow of manure yet displays no sense of conscience vis-à-vis this act (*R* 91). On another occasion, with a marshmallow in his mouth, "he paid a visit to the latrine and there he picked a fight," without provocation (*R* 120). Furthermore, Williams fears all women for the sickness within them. This is hardly testimony to what one critic has called his capability to love (Rechnitz 455).[69] Therefore, to read homosexual desire according to the tropes of nature and culture, innocence, and corruption in *Reflections in a Golden Eye* only ends in the confusion of not only these categories, but also that of heterosexuality/homosexuality, which surreptitiously informs other binaries structuring desire in McCullers's texts. There is no simple distinction between the innocent and the corrupt—heterosexual or homosexual, lover or beloved—as the seemingly simple opposition of nature/culture gives way. Again, we are witness to McCullers's bold project of imagining other forms of relationship outside the more common structural elements.

Other images that expand on that of nature and culture are the depictions of the homosexual as childlike or dandified, or both. The former suggests, like the trope of innocence, a stunted or arrested development. The latter, the dandy, enforces the decadence theme of civilization as well as confronts the simple gender dichotomy of masculine/feminine. That McCullers links homosexuality with childishness is clear in her outline of *The Heart Is a Lonely Hunter*: Lily Mae Jenkins is a "homosexual" whose "mind and feelings are childish" ("Author's Outline" 151). Freudian psychoanalysis, not unproblematically, makes a similar connection, locating the origins of the anal and oral eroticism of homosexuality in infantile sexuality (see Silverman 359).[70] This accords with the claim that the homosexual "is ill in much the same way as a dwarf is ill—because he has never developed" (Clifford Allen, quoted in Sinfield 162), an attitude evoked by the figures of the jockey, Bitsy Barlow, and the dwarf, Cousin Lymon.

It is usually the beloved in McCullers's texts who is childlike. Antonapoulos provides a good example of the beloved-as-child. He is a spoiled brat who treats Singer as his slave. He lives to eat, drink, and sleep (*H* 8), and he is childishly rude (*H* 178–79) and sulky (*H* 10). Like a child, he sticks out his tongue at Singer (*H* 194) and enjoys Mickey Mouse movies (*H* 196). Williams is also childlike, as evidenced in his association with nature, his amorality, and his instinctive mentality. He has a boyish pageboy haircut (*R* 8, 94), does "not smoke, drink, fornicate, nor gamble" (*R* 8), and eats candy in bed (*R* 9).

Besides this direct problematic association of infantilism with homosexuality, which characterizes McCullers's beloveds, there arises the related conceit of the knowing homosexual man who is the corrupter of the ignorant straight boy. This motif of corruption, associated with homoeroticism, comes to the fore in its expression of decadence, often shorthand for homosexuality. Decadence suggests both a moral and cultural degeneration or deterioration, and is also the name of that fin de siècle movement in Europe associated with dandyism and, of course, the most infamous homosexual dandy of all, Oscar Wilde. The dandy plays with feminine artifice and theatricality and so functions as violence against nature. A key element in the common theme of homosexual corruption, then, is femininity. The effeminate Wildean image of the queer was supposedly anathema to Americans because the idea of luxury and leisure is "unAmerican," something associated with England and Europe (Sinfield 154). When the dandy appears in McCullers's works, as either lover or beloved, his figure is troubling, for "he pursues an ideal of charm and personal beauty which the dominant culture, against which he poses himself, labels feminine" (Feldman 3).

Captain Penderton, associated with culture and civilization, affects such a dandy code. He wears a suit "of heavy Chinese silk. . . . The Captain . . . on all social occasions among other officers . . . affected mufti and was a great swell" (*R* 14). He is "keenly sensitive to luxury and a finicky dresser" (*R* 123).[71] Cousin Lymon is also a bit of a swell, in "red and black checkered shirt belonging to Miss Amelia. He did not wear trousers such as ordinary men are meant to wear but a pair of tight-fitting little knee-length breeches" with stockings, "queerly shaped" shoes, and "a shawl of lime-green wool" (*B* 24). But it is not just the lover or the homosexual who appears as the dandy: the eunuch-like Anacleto, who walks "with grace and composure," dresses "in sandals, soft grey trousers, and a blouse of aquamarine linen" (*R* 40) and, on another occasion, an "orange velvet jacket" (*R* 61). He loves ballet, attempts to speak French (*R* 41), and fusses over minute household details (*R* 42–43).

In the figure of the simpleton, Antonapoulos, McCullers presents a grotesque parody of the flippant and witty Wildean dandy. Antonapoulos is fleshy and indulges a passion for sensuous pleasures: "excepting drinking and a certain solitary secret pleasure, Antonapoulos loved to eat more than anything else in the world" (*H* 8). He recalls Charles Baudelaire's dandy who, newly resident in the "New World," is in "the perpetual pursuit of happiness" (26). And Antonapoulos dresses accordingly: in the asylum hospital he wears "a scarlet silk dressing gown and green silk pyjamas and a turquoise ring." "The splendor of his friend's raiment startled [Singer]. . . . The great pulpy folds of his abdomen showed beneath his silk pyjamas" (*H* 194).

The figure of the dandy engages well with the problem of the alleged misogyny implicit in representations of homosexuality in McCullers's writings, for example, the men's seeming flight from grotesque womanhood. For, while seeming to revile women, the homosexual man often makes use of so-called feminine traits. The association between femininity and homosexuality is of course not unique to McCullers's representations of perverseness.[72] Male homosexuality is culturally associated with effeminacy, a supposition that derives from Karl Heinrich Ulrich's formulation of the homosexual as "really" a woman's soul trapped in a man's body. Although, as I discuss in detail in the following chapter on gender performance, all gender in McCullers's texts is potentially transitive, the association of homosexuality with effeminacy is perhaps yet another type of homosexual coding employed by a writer at a time when such a subject was likely to be censored and to provoke social outrage; it also points to the difficulty of imagining other forms of desire without resorting to dangerous stereotype. Not only does dandyism in McCullers's texts mark the homosexual as a grotesque "other" through his association with femininity, but as a figure of decadence, it also suggests the feminine quality of contamination of both the individual and society with which homosexuality is so often crudely charged.

The association of femininity and homosexuality appears more boldly in McCullers's description of the homosexual Lily Mae Jenkins: "When he were younger . . . he were all the time dressing up in girls' clothes" ("Author's Outline" 152). In *The Member of the Wedding* (and not *The Heart Is a Lonely Hunter* as initially planned), Lily Mae again dresses like a girl. Berenice tells Frankie that "Lily Mae fell in love with a man . . . and turned into a girl" (96). In Berenice's formulation, perverse desire is equated with perverse gender. However, as previously indicated, gender and sexuality in McCullers's texts are not as clearly aligned as Berenice imagines.[73]

There are other examples of homosexual effeminacy in McCullers's "almost gay" novels. As I have already suggested, Penderton cannot maintain the phallicization of his virile body as he becomes "infected" with his own perverse desire, so that even his voice, like the Jockey's ("Jockey" 108), becomes "high-pitched" (*R* 66). Lymon appears as a foolish flirtatious woman (*B* 60) in his relationship with Marvin Macy, who is in turn "unimpressed" by the dwarf's antics. Even the hyperbolically virile body of Marvin Macy must come under suspicion. His intense pursuit of masculinity seems to bear out Lacan's claim that "virile display in the human being itself [seems] feminine" (291).[74]

On a first reading then, *Reflections in a Golden Eye* and *The Heart Is a Lonely Hunter* seem to construct homosexuality as a corrupting threat to the innocent and the natural. However, on closer examination, McCullers's engagement with the knotty binary, straight/queer, is made more complex by the fact that even those male characters classified as heterosexual, childlike, and/or natural are "perverse," a perversity that frequently manifests itself in terms of the grotesque feminization of the ideal male body. Major Langdon and Captain Penderton touch on male feminization in a discussion concerning the potential benefits of Anacleto's joining the army. Major Langdon tells the Captain: "'In the army they would have run [Anacleto] ragged and he would have been miserable, but even that seems to me better than *the other*.' 'You mean,' Captain Penderton said, 'that any fulfilment obtained at the expense of normalcy is wrong. . . . In short, it is better, because it is morally honorable, for the square peg to keep scraping about the round hole rather than to discover and use the unorthodox square that would fit it?'" (*R* 112). What causes "moral dishonor," then, is the pursuit of the "unorthodox square."[75]

The unorthodox square might invoke the rectum as the site that affects the feminizing corruption of the masculine self. I suggested earlier that the "rien à voir" of grotesque woman functions in much ultimately misogynist cultural discourse as the "grave" of the male subject. Not only does the vagina-wound supposedly reveal the female's castration as well as threatening the male's, but it is also culturally construed in orthodox heterosexual relations as the site of woman's penetration by the man: she is the passive receiver, while he is the active "doer."[76] It is possible to read the rectum in some forms of homosexual desire in a similar way. That is to say, it might allow entry into what was considered an ideal, impenetrable, self-contained, active body. At this level, then, the homosexual body recalls the grotesque feminine body: open-ended, permeable, soft.

In *Reflections in a Golden Eye,* although Captain Penderton is often described as "rigid as a ramrod," "he was known to the soldiers as Captain Flap-Fanny." Viewed from behind, "his buttocks spread and jounced flabbily in the saddle" (27). These phrases prompt speculation about the metaphorical puncturing and softening of Penderton's stiff body, made accessible, oddly, by his *own* homoerotic desire.[77] It is not only the lover who is a target of the menace of homosexual feminization. Antonapoulos's body is similarly soft, flaccid, and fleshy, like the stereotypical female body: his "huge buttocks would sag down over his plump little feet" (*H* 10). Male same-sex passion, therefore, risks turning the stiff phallic body into a permeable "Flap-Fanny," into grotesque feminization, signaling the instability of bodily bounds and limits. As I explore in depth in the following chapters, femininity as well as masculinity remain intriguing sites of resistance and contradiction in the battle for new ways of living and new worlds.

McCullers's texts are plagued with a struggle to realize the vision of such worlds. At some moments, she seems to be reinstating some form of hierarchical structure of gender and sexuality, as well as casting homosexuality in terms of hackneyed stereotype; at other moments, she launches a potentially fatal challenge to orthodox readings of bodily subjects and politics. For example, while masculinity seems to be favored over femininity in her texts, she reveals the powerful and pervasive force that femininity exacts on all subjects. I, for one, have been forced to wonder how McCullers's fascination with homosexuality impacts her novels. First, it reveals that for McCullers, neither homosexuality nor heterosexuality is ideal or "normal"—all subject positions and all desires are haunted by intriguing oddities and strangenesses; they are grotesque. Second, McCullers's highly intricate portrayal of homosexuality demands that we think about homosexuality as a *productive* mode, in its creation of new pleasures and new relations to others and the world. Finally, the intricacies and unresolved questions that McCullers explores urgently engage with the complex politics of gender and sexuality that still haunt us today.

3
The Masquerade

The Heart Is a Lonely Hunter, The Member of the Wedding, and *The Ballad of the Sad Café*

I have suggested in the previous discussions of embodiment and sexuality that gender in McCullers's fictional worlds is nomadic. But how does this dynamic work? McCullers employs the powerful trope of the masquerade to explore such nomadism, in terms of both the *suspension* and the *foregrounding* of gendering practices.[1] Suspension, specifically of hierarchic categories, is an effect of cross-dressing and transvestism, where the dress of the "other" gender is worn. The foregrounding of gender processes is the exaggerated mimicry of one's "own" gender, normally understood as natural. Both tactics—suspension and foregrounding—resist the normalizing effects of "appropriate" gendering and thus challenge notions of gender as essential and natural.

In *Rabelais and His World,* Bakhtin writes that "[t]he mask . . . rejects conformity to oneself [and] is related to metamorphoses, the violation of natural boundaries [and] to mockery. . . . [S]uch manifestations as parodies, caricatures [and] eccentric postures . . . derived from the mask. It reveals the essence of the grotesque" (40). The image of the masquerade is linked with the fashioning of the self. For instance, in the nineteenth century, literary images of the mask as cross-dressing were related to a romantic yearning after a prelapsarian androgyny. In the twentieth century, Virginia Woolf's *Orlando* and other modernist texts played with the notion of the fluidity of gender positioning: in *Orlando,* for example, the dictum is that one can change selves as one might clothes. Sartorial transgression[2] is a strategic and liberating gesture for women in particular. Sandra Gilbert argues that the image of costume is a powerful expression of and yearning after a fluidity of gender for women writers, since clothing is strongly implicated in the different modes of women's oppression (391–417).

Although there are no literal masquerade scenes in any of McCullers's novels, the claim that it is clothes that make the man (and woman) holds, and this is a concept that would have been particularly attractive to a female writer like the "invert,"[3] Carson McCullers, living and writing in an era where images of the southern belle along with a strong patriarchal society were obstacles in the path of female development, particularly intellectual development. A resulting anxiety over gender could well express itself in the literary trope of gender as masquerade. The homosexual Lily Mae Jenkins, who "changed his nature and his sex and turned into a girl" (M 96), succinctly expresses this gender transitivity.

Both transvestism and cross-dressing underline the concept of gender transitivity and figure prominently in the portrayals of Mick Kelly, Frankie Addams, Miss Amelia Evans, and Biff Brannon. While Biff cross-dresses sporadically and privately, the females' transvestism is sustained and public. Both transvestism and cross-dressing in McCullers's texts suspend gender categories but in different ways. The female characters resist being gendered in terms of *either* feminine *or* masculine, while Biff enacts a type of ritual re-creation of, or search for, an ideal whole self.

At other times, gender in McCullers's texts is produced as *deliberate* masquerade, that is, as the self-conscious wearing of one's own appropriate gender: the female who performs femininity and the male who performs masculinity. Masquerade in this sense, as theater and irony, draws on the subversive concept of mimicry. The male masquerader of masculinity, however, is less susceptible than the feminine female to this sort of strategy since, in McCullers's texts, femininity appears as the more spectacular gender and, consequently, is more amenable to parody. This deliberate type of masquerade *foregrounds* gender operations and its performance, and so tests the supposedly inherent nature of gender.

Opposed to this mimetic performance of correct gender, but drawing on it, is "normal" femininity, or the ideal image of woman. "Proper" femininity is performative, argues Judith Butler, since it involves the repetition of certain acts and gestures that cohere within the received norms of gender identity. This is what women must do to participate properly in society. What emerges from McCullers's texts, particularly *The Heart Is a Lonely Hunter, The Ballad of the Sad Café*, and *The Member of the Wedding*, is the notion that all gender, whether consciously performative or not, is technology.

SUSPENSION: TRANSVESTISM AND CROSS-DRESSING

As I have suggested, there is an attraction for women in the association of identity and costume. In the transvestite figures of McCullers's three tomboys, Frankie Addams, Mick Kelly, and Miss Amelia, the freedom associated with sustained cross-dressing, that is, transvestism, lies in the suspension of normative practices that gender imposes. Such suspension is best expressed in Biff Brannon's vision at the close of *The Heart Is Lonely Hunter:* he is "suspended between radiance and darkness. Between bitter irony and faith" (312). Similarly suspended between the "irony" of gender displacement and the "faith" of an essential gendered identity, the figure of the tomboy overrides categories of either masculine or feminine.

The younger tomboys, Mick Kelly and Frankie Addams, belong to the southern tradition of tomboys. When Mick first enters the narrative, she is described as a "gangling, towheaded youngster, a girl of about twelve . . . [who] was dressed in khaki shorts, a blue shirt, and tennis shoes" (*H* 20). Except for the feminine pronouns that describe Mick throughout the text (and her later forays into femininity), there is not much else to signal to the reader that Mick is a she. For, like Frankie, Mick wishes she were a boy. Accordingly, both girls dress in undershirts and shorts (*H* 20; M 8). Frankie's "hair had been cut like a boy's" (M 8) and, seen through the eyes of the cross-dressing Biff Brannon, Mick "was like a very young boy" (*H* 20). Mick Kelly is exempted from typing classes at school and instead takes mechanical shop "like a boy" (*H* 94), and Frankie is "the best knife thrower in this town" (M 45). Furthermore, as I noted in chapter 1, the young girls' male names reflect their desire to be boys.

Within the fictional worlds of Carson McCullers, it is not difficult to see why the young girls favor male names and costume. To be like a man means to *present* oneself and to be assertive. In contrast, most of McCullers's feminine females are depicted as plain silly and, at best, dull. Accordingly, Mick's older sisters, Etta and Hazel, grate: "Etta was like she was full of worms. . . . Hazel . . . was good-looking but thick in the head." Mick declares that she would "rather be a boy any day" than be like her sisters (*H* 40–41). In *The Member of the Wedding,* Frankie's only experiences of femininity are the husband-obsessed Berenice, Alexandre Dumas's Camille (118), Jarvis's fiancée, Janice, and the neighborhood girls' club.

In comparison, the lives of the girls' male counterparts are truly enviable. Mick's older brother, Bill, "had the nicest room of the family" (*H* 41) and leads a life of minor adventure, "out fishing in the woods, to the clubhouses he built with other boys, to the slot machine in the back of Mr Brannon's restaurant" (*H* 45). Her friend, Harry Minowitz, is able to both work part-time and attend school. Mick realizes that "the're [*sic*] not jobs like that for girls. When a girl wants a job she has to quit school and work full time" (*H* 216), which Mick eventually does. It is no wonder then that the girls cross-identify in the hope of gaining the freedom they see paraded before them every day in terms of "being a man."

In their desire for alternative modes of being, the tomboys are analogous to the "unruly woman" of early literary and festive carnivalesque forms, who functioned as "a multivalent image that could operate . . . to widen behavioral options for women within and even outside marriage. . . . Play with the unruly woman is partly a chance for temporary release from the traditional and stable hierarchy" (N. Davis 131). Through their gender insubordination, then, Mick and Frankie unsettle the status quo of the southern patriarchs; they unsettle the seemingly easy distinction between feminine and masculine that underpins stable gender identity. The girls are thus freaks because to be improperly gendered is to be less than human (see Butler, *Bodies That Matter* 7–8); every human must be either masculine or feminine. In attempting to be like boys, the young girls defy this binarism; they are suspended.

In the end, however, the boyishness of young Mick and Frankie is not so terribly threatening to gender norms, since their boyishness can be construed as merely a phase. As it turns out, their hopes and dreams of new ways of becoming, outside rigid boundaries of identity, are all but stamped out when the tomboys are forced to renounce their masculinity and take up their positions as women. Mick's and Frankie's experiences are typical of female initiation stories: "[S]o many of the young girls . . .

are, at first, dressed in boys' clothing or bear boys' names, attributes they drop as the stories progress. They begin . . . as little androgynous creatures, changing their names and their clothing only as they become aware of their approaching womanhood" (Ginsberg 31).

It is Miss Amelia Evans, the grownup tomboy of *The Ballad of the Sad Café*, who threatens more seriously a status quo based on clear gender demarcation. Like her younger counterparts, Amelia masquerades as a man to avoid the fate of the women around her and to enjoy the relative freedoms of the life of men. Her masculine masquerade, it could be said, is a lifestyle choice; it is not a temporary performance. It is, ironically, her femininity that is a mask to be worn or taken off at will.

Like the young girls, Miss Amelia is exceedingly tall (20), has short-cropped hair (20), and wears "overalls and gumboots" (9). She is a hard-working laborer, a good fighter, and has a "passion for lawsuits and the courts" (9). An astute businesswoman, she runs a successful café and operates a still that produces "the best liquor in the county" (8). Amelia both looks and behaves like a man and so has access to the world of men. As such, in her creation of new currents of power and her destabilization of gender norms, she is seen as a threat to the overwhelmingly male community in which she moves. Amelia is the embodiment of a female power Westling sees lurking behind the southern patriarchs' idealization of "weakness" in the southern lady (17).[4]

Miss Amelia has most frequently been characterized as an Amazon.[5] The Amazons lived by "spurning men, tracking game, rejoicing in battle, inverting biology and flouting nature." Tales of the Amazons, "devourers" of men, conclude with their slaughter by male enemies (Warner 204).[6] This brief description maps Miss Amelia's fate. Amelia is a good fighter, her manliness inverts biology and flouts nature, and, for one reader at least, she is a devourer of men: she is "almost monstrous, the female who preys upon the male [Marvin Macy] whom she has lured to her abode" (McDowell 68). Finally, Amelia is conquered by her male enemies, Cousin Lymon and Marvin Macy. The only element that perhaps separates Amelia from her Amazon ancestors is that she spurns not only men but also women.

Most significantly, the Amazon, associated as she is with the deathly "closed womb" (Warner 205), is usually a virgin as is Miss Amelia. Her relationship with Cousin Lymon is asexual, resembling that of mother and child. Lymon "is a man loved without sex, a child acquired without pain and a companion which [Miss Amelia's] limited personality finds more acceptable than a husband or a child" (Millichap, *Carson McCullers* 335). Since their relationship is set up as that between mother and child, physical union between Amelia and Cousin Lymon would amount to incest, the greatest of taboos.

Furthermore, on the night of Amelia's marriage to Marvin Macy, "the bride went about her ordinary business—reading the newspaper, finishing an inventory of the stock in the store, and so forth. . . . At eleven o'clock the bride took a lamp and went upstairs. The groom followed close behind her. . . . [W]hat followed after was unholy. Within half an hour Miss Amelia had stomped down the stairs in breeches and a khaki jacket. Her face had darkened so that it looked quite black. . . . She poked up the fire, sat down, and . . . read *The Farmer's Almanac*, . . . and had a smoke with her father's pipe. . . . That was the way in which she spent the whole of her wedding night" (38–39). And so it continues for three days until Miss Amelia and Marvin Macy come to blows and Amelia finally kicks him out.

It is clear that Amelia sees no necessary connection between the wedding ceremony and its consummation. Similarly, Frankie Addams, in her wish to join her brother's wedding, does not consider the sexual implications of doing so. Moreover, to repeat, Frankie's plan to join the wedding is a means of avoiding sexual relations, which she sees as tied up with her impending womanhood. Like Amelia, when dressed as a boy Frankie avoids adult sexuality. It is when she dresses as a female, as the girlish "F. Jasmine," that she has her frightening experience with the soldier. Significantly, while the narrator of *The Ballad of the Sad Café* considers Amelia's sexual rejection of Marvin Macy "unholy," for Frankie, it is the sexual act itself, not its rejection, which is an evil: she refers to "the unknown sin" committed with Barney MacKean (*M* 33). Frightened by what she has seen or experienced, she tries to "forget," just as she does after witnessing her father's two boarders having a "common fit" (*M* 50).

Mick Kelly's sexual experience with Harry Minowitz leaves her feeling similarly fearful and vulnerable, convinced that "[s]he was a grown person now, whether she wanted to be or not" (*H* 243). It seems that it is sexual intercourse that makes Mick a "woman," just as her graffiti "PUSSY" positioned her as a commodity in the heterosexual marketplace.[7] Her anatomy marks her gender, which is the very thing her boyish appearance seeks to veil.

Frankie's fear and "forgetting," Berenice's harping on about "white boy beaus," and Mick's scrawling of "PUSSY" and her first sexual experience all reflect the observation that for the young girl, puberty—and thus womanliness—"is not figured as the coming of a self-chosen maturity but as the signal of immanent reproductive capacities" (Grosz, *Volatile Bodies* 205). And so the townsfolk hope that marriage will turn Miss Amelia "at last into a calculable woman" (*B* 38). It seems that it is the sex act that makes a girl, even a tomboy, a woman. Thus, to reject heterosexual relations is to freakishly reject being gendered "woman."

Some readers see reflected in Amelia's rejection of Marvin Macy her *fear* of heterosexual relations. Accordingly, she is fearful, a failure, or representative of an unfulfilled subjectivity,[8] and heterosexuality is equated with a full and healthy feminine identity. These interpretations of the manly Miss Amelia's rejection of genital sexuality recall Riviere's discussion of a woman who suffers from a "great anxiety about defloration." Riviere concludes that this particular woman "was afraid of impotence in exactly the same way as a man. . . . It was a determination not to be beaten by the man." In analysis, the woman's "mask of womanliness was being peeled away, and she was revealed as either castrated, . . . or as wishing to castrate" (38–39). Similarly, the consummation of Miss Amelia and Marvin Macy's marriage might potentially castrate the masculine woman, revealing what lies "behind the mask" of her manliness, namely, her lack, her "not all there," her "not quite there" (Cixous 49). Thus, the sexual act might be disempowering for the woman since it castrates her to reveal and thus confirm her lack. This analysis, however, is problematic to say the least. Not only does it privilege the phallus in a consideration of subjectivity and sexuality, but it also falls into the trap of "the old feminine metaphor of the truth as (of) unveiling" (Spivak, "Displacement" 174–75). For, it is upon the *surface* that gender identity is forcefully mapped and played out. To reject the dynamic of unveiling and castration leads to an alternative, more affirmative reading of the females' supposedly unfeminine dismissal of heterosexuality.

Freud sets out three options for the development of the little girl: a "normal" femininity, which means she accepts her castration; a "masculinity complex," whereby she refuses castration; or "frigidity," the rejection of sexual relations. This last position is a more subversive one since it can undermine traditional encounters between men and women in its refusal of male-defined forms of pleasure. Further, in light of the female transvestism under discussion here, there is a link also between frigidity, or more properly virginity, and the "masculinity complex." For a woman, to act like a man might mean the maintenance of virginity. So, the choices appear to be (feminine) acceptance of male-centered desire or (masculine) virginity.

The descriptions of costume in *The Heart Is a Lonely Hunter, The Ballad of the Sad Café*, and *The Member of the Wedding* clearly reflect this polarization of possible alternatives for female identity. Miss Amelia wears either overalls or a red dress and wedding dress. The red dress suggests prostitution and the wedding dress, maidenhood. In *The Heart Is a Lonely Hunter*, as Mick dreams of one day conducting an orchestra, she thinks "she would wear either a real man's evening suit or a red dress spangled with rhinestones" (212). When Frankie plans to run away after the "nightmare" of the wedding, she decides either to get a job in Hollywood as a "starlet" or to "dress like a boy . . . and join the Marines" (M 175). In all three instances, the choice is made clear: to be like a man or to be a sexual object.

However, more is achieved, or at least attempted, in the masculinity of McCullers's tomboys. Rather than merely being a part of the machinery of gender division, the tomboys, both young and old, *suspend* such categories. For to be *like* a man is not to *be* a man. In refusing gender categories, the tomboys also call into question what it means to be human, if being human is to be gendered as either masculine or feminine.

The suspension of either/or identity categories might be appealing to women, who are culturally associated with, and marked and defined as, lack. Doane usefully writes that "the woman becomes the man in order to attain the necessary distance from the image" of woman (82). In doing so, she becomes neither masculine nor feminine. Because it is the sexual act (whose ideal function is to make the tomboys "women") that embodies the threat or reality of the fall into the division of either/or gender categories, by rejecting sexual intercourse the tomboys seek a prelapsarian state of ambivalence outside dichotomous representation. Both Frankie's reference to her experience with Barney MacKean as "sin" as well as the narrator's view of Miss Amelia's dealings with Marvin Macy as "unholy" suggest the gravitas of what is at stake in the politics of the sexual act.

So, a dynamic of masculinity-virginity-suspension is at work in the tomboys of McCullers's texts and not the less viable one of castration. As a result of their resistance to cultural norms, the tomboys must be either turned back from their unnatural ways (as Frankie and Mick are) or punished (as Miss Amelia is). Anyway, heterosexual genital sexual relations might not be in the tomboys' repertoire at all. That is, their desire might fall outside of male-defined forms of pleasure. In fact, I would agree with Westling, who writes that *The Ballad of the Sad Café* as a whole reveals "McCullers's complete rejection of heterosexual union" (125).

Mannish and virginal, the adult Miss Amelia empowers herself as she maintains her ambiguity. In consequence, her forsaken husband, the humiliated and castrated Marvin Macy, seeks retribution. Again, this scenario recalls Riviere's analysis of the woman who, in her desire to possess "the invincible sword . . . [renders] powerless and helpless (her gentle husband)" (42). On a more general level, the new form of power Miss Amelia creates through transvestism and the refusal of normative demarcations must be contained. In passing beyond puberty, the ritual of the adolescent's inscription of femininity (or masculinity), the grownup Amelia is particularly upsetting to what might be thought of as the natural order of things.

It would make sense then to read the fight scene at the ballad's conclusion as Marvin Macy's final defloration of Miss Amelia (Gilbert and Gubar 109–10), thus casting her on the side of "woman." Her "defloration" leaves her sobbing and feeble (*B* 81). "[H]er body shrank until she was thin as old maids are thin when they go crazy" and "[h]er voice was broken, soft, and sad" (*B* 83). McCullers's portrait of Miss Amelia would seem to reinforce the claim that gender has to do with power relations: to be weak is to be feminine and to be strong is to be masculine (Robinson 77). Amelia's power is broken as she is turned into "woman," a suitable punishment for one who resists taking up the appropriate role and thus violates natural boundaries. Like the carnivalesque unruly woman,

Amelia is allowed "a temporary period of dominion, which is ended only after she has said or done something to undermine authority or denounce its abuse" (N. Davis 135).

Certainly, Miss Amelia is beaten by the "betweenness of men," that is, the conspiracy of Cousin Lymon and Marvin Macy, but it is important to bear in mind why she *has* to be beaten. Like her younger though less dangerous counterparts, the figure of the transvestic Miss Amelia upsets the bounds of appropriate gendered behavior; she unsettles normative configurations of identity upon which the status quo is dependent. In her sustained cross-dressing, Miss Amelia creates a resistance so great that she must be contained, and this is reified in the image of the boarded-up café: "The building looks completely deserted. Nevertheless, on the second floor there is one window which is not boarded; sometimes in the late afternoon . . . a hand will slowly open the shutter and a face will look down. . . . It is a face like the terrible dim faces known in dreams" (*B* 7). Amelia is left a "woman, gender-locked in a decaying house" (Kahane, "Gothic Mirror" 348). However, there is nonetheless a remnant of power in this image of Miss Amelia, as she looks *down* on the town. Furthermore, femininity (Amelia's appropriate gender), which I consider in a following section, proves to be as controversial and as unsubstantiating as transvestism. It is difficult to pin down any sense of true womanliness or, for that matter, manliness in McCullers's texts. In wanting to be men, the tomboys suspend these facile gender categories. In this respect, the transvestism of the tomboys, particularly the adult Amelia, does not simply fail. It is, rather, *too much*.

It is not only women in McCullers's texts who cross over to the other gender through both dress and behavior. However, when Biff Brannon takes up the costume of the other, he does so as a temporary tactic, unlike the sustained transvestism of Mick Kelly, Frankie Addams, Miss Amelia Evans, and even Lily Mae Jenkins. Just as pertinently, Biff, McCullers's principal male cross-dresser, performs femininity *in private*. As such, his transgression is not susceptible to the societal pressure or punishment to which the females are exposed. Biff Brannon's cross-dressing, safely done in the bedroom before the mirror, becomes a private meditation on the self and its metamorphic possibilities and lacks the social commentary and prospective upheaval the women's transvestism provokes.

Another difference between Biff and the other characters who cross over to perform the other gender involves the question of the specularity of the gendered performance in question. I return to this, but it should be noted here that femininity is generally construed as the more spectacular gender, constructed as it is as an artifact in terms of accessorization. The example of John Henry of *The Member of the Wedding* bears out this claim.

John Henry, Frankie's young cousin, plays with a doll and dresses as a woman: "[H]e had put on Berenice's hat and was trying to walk in Berenice's high-heeled shoes" (133). Another time he wears Frankie's jonquil dress to resemble "a little old woman dwarf" (145–46). John Henry's drag, however, is not so unsettling. First, he is still too young to bother the world with it, unlike Amelia and even her young counterparts. Second, his cross-dressing seems unmotivated, again unlike the females whose manliness promises freedom and independence. John Henry's womanly dressing is but a game, make-believe. At most, it points out that each time a woman presents "true" femininity, she is performing the feminine masquerade.

Like John Henry, the homosexual Lily Mae Jenkins, "[w]hen he were younger . . . were all the time dressing up in girls' clothes" and "[e]verybody thought he were real cute then" ("Author's Outline" 152). However, like Miss Amelia Evans and her masquerade of manliness, Lily Mae, wearing a "pink satin blouse" (M 96), continues his feminine masquerade into adulthood when he appears in *The Member of the Wedding*. Berenice tells Frankie that he "turned into a girl. . . . To all intents and purposes." "Cute" when young, Lily Mae, as the adult transvestite, becomes one "of many a queer thing" of which Berenice has heard (96).

Most significantly, Lily Mae's feminine masquerade signals his homosexuality. Both his femininity, suggested as much by his clothing as by his childishness, and his homosexuality, discussed in the previous chapter, are wholly appropriate for one whose love-object is a man. In this instance, then, Lily Mae's transvestism, which suggests his womanly identification, works to undermine not only neat categories of gender but also those of sexuality, particularly heterosexual organization. Like the tomboys, he is an example of the improperly gendered freak.

Biff Brannon is perhaps a more complex masquerader of femininity. While Lily Mae's masquerade of femininity signals his homosexuality,

Biff's signals his "true" self.[9] To express this true self, Biff appropriates his dead wife's traits. For, while Alice was alive, she "always made him feel different from his real self" (*H* 17). On her death, he puts her lemon rinse through his hair and her perfume "on his dark, hairy armpits. . . . He exchanged a deadly secret glance with himself in the mirror and stood motionless" (*H* 198). Biff's true feminized self is potentially "deadly" before the gaze. It seems that Biff is well aware of the social risks of performing this new self in public.

That Biff feels his *real* self is able to be expressed through *masquerade* is worthy of comment. There could in fact be no intrinsically real or fixed self expressed here, feminine or otherwise, since it is cosmetics—perfume and hair rinse—that construct this self. It is not natural, nor is it inherent. Biff's new surroundings further underscore the manufactured nature of Biff's real and feminine self. After Alice's death, he redecorates the bedroom in decadent opulence: "[T]here was a thick red rug on the floor, and he had bought a beautiful cloth of Chinese blue to hang on the side of the wall. . . . Blue silk cushions were on the studio couch, and he had [made] deep red curtains for the window. . . . It was both luxurious and sedate. On the table there was a little Japanese pagoda" (*H* 198). Thus, it appears Biff's real self is something that can be assembled and projected onto his environment, something he can take up and then discard at will. It may be a secret, private self, but it is not an authentic self. Although Biff claims that his self *is* his truth, it is the very masquerade itself that produces this true self. In the figure of Biff Brannon, authenticity and constructedness come to be one and the same thing.

Biff himself offers an insight into his initial rejection (sexual and otherwise) of his wife and his subsequent appropriation of her femininity on her death. He considers that perhaps "the one who has gone is not really dead, but grows and is created for a second time in the soul of the living" (*H* 111).[10] He incorporates a lost femininity, represented by the death of his wife.[11] Thus, the text acknowledges the other, in this instance femininity, which is excluded for the sake of a stable masculine identity. Furthermore, Biff's taking up of Alice's femininity is a kind of becoming-other of self, in the same way that I suggested narcissism might be in the previous chapter. In this respect, Biff's crossing over to femininity is a creative and productive process and echoes Bakhtin's claim that the mask enables a rejection of "conformity to oneself" (*Rabelais* 40). Again, as with the tomboys, the result is a suspension of strictly demarcated gender identity.

Biff's position in and before the mirror is on first consideration an enclosed narcissistic one. He is at once object and subject of the gaze. This proximity is enhanced by the fact that object and subject are both feminine. Thus, spectator and image are identified. In this way, Biff experiences a sense of completion. Naturally reminded of Alice in the transvestic moment before the mirror, he feels that "now their life together was whole as only the past can be whole." But there is a stasis in this Oneness. As he glances sideways at himself, he senses "[t]he boundary of death" (*H* 198). The self folds in on itself to dissolve any concept of subjectivity.

However, while gazing in the mirror and wearing Alice's scent, Biff "stiffens" and finally turns away "abruptly" (*H* 198).[12] It seems that a rupture of the deathly Oneness takes place. There is no clear evidence in the text to explain Biff's reaction, but I would suggest that Biff experiences if not a split then an *unfixed* self, perhaps in the very realization of the manufactured nature of his "real" self. He becomes the masculine subject gazing upon a feminine self, which is then foregrounded and divested of its truth. Linked with this is Biff's possible acknowledgment of his self-degrading movement toward womanliness.

Biff invests heavily in a constructed self, and thus his subsequent awakening to the fact is marked by horror. The moment of recognition takes place before the mirror, signaling to Biff his "real" self as disguise and his degradation. It is the flat plane that reveals the true/disguised self, further emphasizing that gender identity is a form of surfacial masquerade. Accordingly, Biff's transvestism should be looked *at*, not *through*, for it is on the surface that the workings of gender play themselves out.

FOREGROUNDING: "CALCULABLE" MEN AND WOMEN

Psychoanalytic discourse frequently conceives of an individual's own gender also as masquerade. Riviere, in her 1929 essay "Womanliness as a Masquerade," claims that it is specifically women's womanliness that is equated with masquerade since womanliness masks a masculinity basic to all human subjects. Having argued that "women who wish for masculinity may put on a mask of womanliness to avert anxiety and the retribution feared from men," she then comes to the now infamous conclusion that "genuine womanliness and the 'masquerade' . . . are the same thing" (35, 38). That is to say, for Riviere, there is no womanliness that is not masquerade. Lacan, in "The Signification of the Phallus," argues that *both* feminine and masculine subject positions depend on "feminine" masquerade, feminine since any masquerade has to do with disguise and dissimulation, characteristics problematically associated with femininity. Both men and women must masquerade since the relations between the sexes depend on the woman's *seeming* to "be" the phallus and the man's *seeming* to "have" the phallus (289). Although femininity is the more spectacular gender, Lacan nevertheless claims that "[t]he fact that femininity finds its refuge in this mask . . . has the curious consequence of making virile display in the human being itself seem feminine" (291). Crucially then, the "normal" man, who displays traits that are acceptably masculine, is as much a performer as Riviere's woman.

McCullers's texts represent "feminine" masquerade for men in the form of masculine caricature, that is, in the hyperbolization of what is perceived as a natural and appropriate masculinity. I have already explored this phenomenon in the virile bodies of the homosexual lovers and beloveds in the previous chapter, yet it is also the straight man in McCullers's texts who actually *performs* gender behavior that is supposedly natural to him. Just as the tomboys perform a masculinity, so, too, do the straight men. That this is the case with McCullers's men challenges Riviere's claim that it is femininity alone which is masquerade and hides a "fundamental" masculine nature. For masculinity, too, is a doing, even if it is less spectacular than femininity; masculinity depends on the make-believe of the equation of penis and phallus (Silverman 15).[13]

Marvin Macy, Major Langdon, Jake Blount, and even Biff Brannon offer good examples of the exaggeration of male performance. In his youth, Marvin Macy was "the handsomest man in this region—being six feet one inch, hard-muscled, and with slow grey eyes and curly hair" (*B* 34).[14] And on his return to town, Macy resembles the hyper-masculine image of the cowboy in "a red shirt, and a wide belt of tooled leather; he carried a tin suitcase and a guitar" (*B* 57). He acts tough, swaggering around town with a knife (*B* 61), taking food from his hostess's hungry children as he "settled himself in the best and warmest sleeping place in the front room" (*B* 61–62). He is a *caricature* of ideal American masculinity.

Major Langdon also acts out exaggerated masculinity in *Reflections in a Golden Eye.* An insensitive boor, he is apparently capable of only a few tasks: horse riding, seducing Leonora Penderton (which he compares with "being out on manoeuvres" [49]), and following army orders. One of Langdon's favorite aphorisms is: "'Only two things matter . . . —to be a good animal and to serve my country. A healthy body and patriotism'" (116). Langdon pretends to read "a very recondite and literary book" while secretly engrossed in "a pulp magazine called *Scientification*" about "a wild, interplanetary superwar" (46). His wife, Alison, considers him to be "as stupid and heartless as a man could be" (79). Like Marvin Macy, Langdon is hyperbolically masculine.

Jake Blount of *The Heart Is a Lonely Hunter* is another manly man. In her outline of the story, McCullers writes that "[i]n physique he suggests a stunted giant." A man who attempts to keep "his lips from betraying his emotions," he "depends heavily on alcohol" ("Author's Outline" 143). In the novel itself, he is "a short, squat man in overalls," a fighter "with heavy shoulders like beams," and a boisterous drunk (16). His hands are "huge, stained and calloused" (18) and his jokes "so raw he had to be hushed up with beer" (19). He is so filthy that he smells like a goat (22) when he first comes to town. Alice Brannon, locating him in the realm of masquerade and disguise, describes him as "a spectacle . . . and a circus too." Her husband, Biff, finds that Blount's "moustache looked false, as if it had been stuck on for a costume party and would fall off if he talked too fast" (18). Biff concludes that "Blount was not a freak, although when you first saw him he gave you that impression. It was like something was deformed about him—but when you looked at him closely each part of him was normal and as it ought to be" (22). In Biff's response, Blount appears as a sum of manufactured parts, to be put together or pulled to bits as suggested, for instance, by his seemingly detachable moustache. This is enhanced in a letter Singer writes to Antonapoulos in which he describes Blount: "Sometimes he is dressed in a plain suit, and the next time he will be black with dirt and smelling bad and in the overalls he wears to work. He will shake his fist and say ugly drunken words" (190). Like Woolf's Orlando, who has a wardrobe of selves, Blount has a choice of masculine masks, just as femininity is a choice of types of dress for Miss Amelia and Mick.

Biff Brannon's performance of femininity is also offset by a similarly stereotypical masculinity. The narrator of *The Heart Is a Lonely Hunter* describes him as "a hard man . . . with a beard so dark and heavy that the lower part of his face looked as though it were moulded of iron" (15).[15] With a "wiry-haired chest" (32), his hands are "calloused," like Jake Blount's, and his "eyes were cold and staring" (17).

From this brief examination of Marvin Macy, Major Langdon, Jake Blount, and Biff Brannon, it appears that McCullers's texts more often than not highly exaggerate masculinity to the point of caricature. Masculinity is not original but parodic of some *ideal* and therefore necessarily unattainable origin. Constructed as a type of fetishism, the exaggerated masculinity of these characters suggests a lack, not so much a lack of someone or something behind the mask but of an essential and stable identity. This is what Lacan means by the "femininity" of virile display: it is feminine because, as masquerade, it covers over lack. An analysis of the feminine masquerade performed by woman will highlight more powerfully the fluidity of gender in McCullers's text, showing that for all women, femininity is fabricated.

It is the strategy of *mimicry* that reveals the parodic and performative nature of the more spectacular gender, femininity. Mimicry foregrounds the processes that ideally work to create a stably and intelligibly gendered human subject. Foregrounding creates a gap between form and content, between ideal and practice, "so they appear not as a partnership, but as a warfare, a struggle" (Harpham 7). The practice of feminine mimicry, then, is closely bound up with the ideal image of woman.

The image of woman aligns itself with culturally acceptable femininity. Butler claims that to display one's "normal" gender is "not the product of a choice, but the forcible citation of a norm, whose complex historicity is indissociable from relations of discipline, regulation, and punishment" (*Bodies That Matter* 232).[16] Those whose gender is not readily ascertainable—for instance, Miss Amelia and the young tomboys—are marginalized by and suffer in the face of constricting gender norms; they are considered freaks. Ideal femininity is, in the words of the narrator of Kate Chopin's *The Awakening*, "that fictitious self which we assume like a garment with which to appear before the world" (234). This type of imitative femininity recalls both Riviere's and Lacan's respective conceptualizations of masquerade whereby women must *seem* womanly as a means of either averting male retribution or entering into heterosexual desire. And as Irigaray also claims, it is what women must do to participate in the Symbolic: "[t]he cosmetics, the disguises of all kinds that women cover themselves with are intended to deceive, to promise more value than can be delivered. . . . Is there pleasure in this for women? Not much, not simply" (*Speculum* 114). If they play by the rules, Irigaray says, women achieve femininity, but the masquerade has little to offer women: it may protect them from recrimination or suspicion, but it gives them little pleasure (*This Sex* 133–34).[17]

McCullers's texts provide several examples of this conceptualization of woman. One example is the virgin angel who masks her specific desire. The more powerful but "unfeminine" virgin (usually accused of frigidity) who rejects heterosexual relations and seemingly escapes the fall into gendering has already been considered in this chapter. Of the socially approved feminine virgin, Irigaray notes that "though her body is beautiful and she is decked out in gold for him and by him, woman will still be reserved, modest, shameful, as far as her sex organs are concerned. She will discreetly assist in hiding them. . . . For woman's 'body' has some 'usefulness' . . . only on condition that her sex organs are hidden" (*Speculum* 115). In *Clock Without Hands*, Judge Clane's wife, "Miss Missy"—"[a] purer woman never lived" (49)—typifies virginity figured as ideal femininity.[18] Fittingly, this angel wife, dead mother of one, was a member of the church choir. As if to confirm her virginal status, her breast, a signifier of pleasure, is removed when she is diagnosed with cancer, just as Alison Langdon cuts off her nipple in *Reflections in a Golden Eye*. Miss Missy is also a martyr, for when she "knew she was ill again she wanted to spare her husband the truth" (C 49). As Sherman Pew cannily notes, "every boy's mother is virtuous, especially if she is *imaginary*" (C 146, emphasis added). Here, succinctly put, is the image of the virgin-mother-woman.

In *The Member of the Wedding* and *The Heart Is a Lonely Hunter*, the goodly feminine woman functions as a role model for the recalcitrant young tomboys. These women embody a "normal" femininity effected through accessorization. It soon becomes apparent that "it is necessary to *become* a woman. . . . [For] a woman has to . . . enter into the *masquerade of femininity*" (Irigaray, *This Sex* 134).[19] Etta Kelly provides one such model of femininity for Mick to emulate. "All she thought about was movie stars and getting in the movies. . . . She primped all the day long," looking in the mirror and doing chin exercises (*H* 40). Here, as with Biff's feminine masquerade, the mirror only enhances the spectacular and performative aspects of femininity.

In *The Member of the Wedding,* the girls of the neighborhood clubhouse, who "had parties with boys on Saturday night" (17), represent the feminine stereotype against which Frankie Addams measures herself. Westling writes that they provide "a sublime vision of Frankie–F. Jasmine's destiny, a vision of ideal feminine grace" (128–29). Janice, Frankie's future sister-in-law, also functions as another model of femininity. According to Berenice, Janice looked "natural" (37), "a kind of brunette and small and pretty" (38), unlike the gawky overgrown tomboy. Frankie adds to the picture: "Janice had on a green dress and green high-heel dainty shoes. Her hair was done up in a knot" (38). Janice is one of the prettiest people Frankie has ever seen (38). Again, as in Biff's case, the natural and the artificial come to be as one. Fittingly, Berenice advises Frankie to " 'speak sweetly and act sly' " in order that she might catch a suitable husband (98). To "act sly" is the essence of the deception that, Irigaray claims, women must practice. However, this is also where power may lie: in the exaggeration of womanliness as a mode of production, not as an essentially gendered identity. In this way, not only does "the woman [use] her own body as a disguise" in the masquerade of femininity,[20] but she is also empowered because she is producing *herself* as feminine spectacle.

This second model of womanhood as parody is strategic. Like the mockery reserved for the mask of carnival Bakhtin describes, mimicry highly exaggerates the image of woman to reveal the contradictions inherent in those models which hold that gender is natural and innate. Mimicry stresses the difference between the mimic and what she mimes, that is, the image of woman. Irigaray discusses the concept of mimicry in terms of femininity in *This Sex Which Is Not One;* she imagines a more subversive use of it. One does not have to be simply a "dutiful" mimic, playing "natural": "One must assume the feminine role deliberately. . . . To play with mimesis for a woman is thus, for a woman, to try to recover the place of her exploitation by discourse, without allowing herself to be simply reduced to it" (76). Thus, mimesis is "not a deluded masquerade, but a canny mimicry" (Schor, "This Essentialism" 48), the "bitter irony" to which Biff Brannon alludes (*H* 312) and the very process Frankie, Mick, and Miss Amelia engage in when they act like a woman. In other words, McCullers's texts hyperbolize the masquerade of femininity to such an extent that it becomes a strategic movement outside the bounds of normative gender identity, not an attempt to either participate in male desire or to "avert . . . retribution feared from men" (Riviere 35). Exaggerated femininity reveals supposed subject fundamentals, masculine and feminine, to be manufactured performance.

The parodic possibilities of doing femininity, as opposed to masculinity, are drawn out by femininity's more spectacular nature, stemming from Riviere's equation of womanliness and masquerade, and further suggest that femininity is more closely aligned with display and exhibitionism than is masculinity. Marjorie Garber, in *Vested Interests*, calls woman's spectacular femininity "artifactuality": "woman as artifact [is] assembled from a collection of parts: wig, painted nails, mascara and 'blush'" (49). I will show that it is precisely because womanliness is so visible that the mask of femininity *worn by women* works well to illustrate the parodic and performative nature of all gendered identity figured as natural, original, and beyond the taint of culture. Where transvestism has the effect of suspending categories of stably gendered either/or identity, the performance of the more appropriate gender, in this case femininity, serves to *foreground* technologies of gender.

The parodic portrayal of Baby Wilson of *The Heart Is a Lonely Hunter* well exemplifies the artifactuality of femininity, which in her case is exaggerated to such an extent that it is grotesque. At only four years old Baby Wilson, like Truman Capote's Miss Bobbit in "Children on Their Birthdays," is hideous in her femininity, with her "finger waves" and "her dancing and expression lessons." With her daughter dressed in "a little white dress with white shoes and white socks and even small white gloves," Lucile pinches her "little cheeks to put more color in them." Like a performing circus dog, "[s]he curved both her arms above her head and her feet slid slowly in opposite directions on the yellow waxed floor. . . . She posed with her arms held at a fancy angle" (114). Another time she appears on the street in a little pink tutu: "With her yellow hair she was all pink and white and gold—and so small and clean that it almost hurt to watch her. She prissed across the street in a cute way" (146–47).

Baby Wilson, like Janice, is a miniature of "the little woman" and as such points to the commodification and mass production of women. Feminine and domesticated, and reminiscent of a dainty fairy, Baby is in stark opposition to the unbridled giants, Mick and Frankie. Baby Wilson performs, albeit unwittingly, the parodic masquerade of femininity. In her very specularity, the grotesque Baby is surface not depth, artifice not truth, assemblage not integrity. Again, what is emphasized here is the surfaciality of gender as masquerade, as costume. The figure of Baby Wilson clearly draws on the visibility (Garber's artifactuality) of the feminine image, so that femininity is distanced from the performer to foreground its production as artifice and to reveal it as something to be worn and taken off.

Both Mick and Frankie, as already discussed, reject the models of femininity before them at the start of their respective stories. Mick tells her sisters, "'I don't want to be like either of you. . . . I'd rather be a boy any day'" (*H* 41). Mick's attitude is reflected in the short story "Like That," where the young nameless female protagonist rejects the image of womanhood offered her in the form of her older sister: "You see I'd never be like Sis is now. I don't want to grow up—if it's like that" (86). And Frankie calls the clubhouse girls "sons-of-bitches" (M 18). As preadolescent girls, it is seemingly acceptable for Mick, Frankie, and the young girl of "Like That" to appear as tomboys. However, the young tomboy "must . . . face the fact that grown men and women make love, and that her body makes her desirable to men" (Westling 130).[21]

Eventually, Frankie and Mick, with their feminine role models before them, attempt to avert the disaster that befell the overgrown tomboy of *The Ballad of the Sad Café* by taking up a sort of womanliness. However, in doing so, wittingly or otherwise, they reveal the gendering process to be the very artful game that it is. Westling suggests that when the tomboys do "appear in dress, it is a *deliberate* and very awkward capitulation to social demands for conformity" (177, emphasis added). Westling's choice of "deliberate" is crucial here for it seems that the girls adopt the ultrafeminine stereotype as their role model. Mick first appears in feminine attire at her prom party. She wears "Etta's long blue crêpe de chine evening dress and some white pumps and a rhinestone tiara for her hair" and "one of Etta's brassières just for the heck of it. . . . This was the first time she had ever worn an evening dress." She spends time on her hair and finally "put on plenty of lipstick and paint." Standing before the mirror, Mick decides that "she either looked like a sap or else she looked very beautiful." Whichever, "[s]he didn't feel like herself at all. She was somebody different from Mick Kelly entirely" (*H* 97). Mick's self-perception suggests that the tomboy "Mick Kelly" is some essential self, that is, her boyish self. As in Biff Brannon's case, here it is the other gender that represents the real self. Mick's observation echoes Riviere's argument that femininity is a dissimulation of some fundamental masculinity. However, as was made clear, Mick's masculinity is not only a performative mode, as she also feels her "femininity" is, but it also leads to the *suspension* of such dichotomous gender categories.

Mick unconsciously makes a mockery of womanliness. Once the party is ruined by the neighborhood children, Mick finds she is restricted by her feminine clothes, with the hem of her evening gown now torn and her tiara now lost, and she puts on her old shorts and shirt. However, she finally decides that "[s]he was too big to wear shorts any more after this" (*H* 105) and embarks on further forays into femininity. She begins to wear perfume in case she should meet Mister Singer (*H* 214, 269), and once she starts school, she wears a skirt and blouse (*H* 190) and, on Sundays, a dress of "wine coloured silk with a dingy lace collar" (*H* 205). Again, for the interview at Woolworth's, she wears "Hazel's green silk dress and a green hat and high-heeled pumps with silk stockings." Her sisters "fixed her face with rouge and lipstick and plucked her eyebrows" (*H* 279). Biff, once tantalized by her tomboyishness, notices at the close of the story that "there was something ladylike and delicate about her that was hard to point out. The ear-rings, the dangle of her bracelets, and the new way she crossed her legs and pulled the hem of her skirt down past her knees" (*H* 311). Thus, Mick's approach to womanliness (as well as Biff's response) foregrounds femininity as an assemblage of ultimately deceptive accoutrements and deportment.

Unlike Frankie, who finally reverts to her real name, Frances, Mick does not change her name to reflect her new womanliness. This only serves to emphasize the failure of naming as a device for ensuring properly gendered subjectivity. Furthermore, traces of Mick's earlier tomboyish dress and behavior never quite leave her. Her stockings have runs in them; she sticks chewing gum in them to halt the run (*H* 205, 306). In her school skirt, "the pleats had come out and the hem dragged loose around her sharp jutting knees" (*H* 119). She threatens to "knock down" the men she imagines might come and take Singer's piano from her. These instances do not tally with a newly acquired womanliness. Mick seems only able to *approximate* womanliness, just as she and the other tomboys are only able to approximate manliness.

Mick here resembles the Bakhtinian fool of carnival.[22] The fool or clown is charged with "*not grasping* the conventions of society . . . , not understanding lofty pathos—charged labels, things and events," and so "makes strange the world of conventionality" ("Discourse" 402, 404).[23] In sum, the fool unmasks by a failure to understand, that is, through "stupidity (incomprehension)" ("Discourse" 403). In a similar way, Mick, in her failed attempts to be a woman, reveals the gaps in the ideally seamless mask of femininity.

In *The Member of the Wedding,* Frankie also performs as the fool when she aspires to "womanliness." Berenice observes that Frankie looks incongruous in the gaudy orange satin dress she has chosen for the wedding. It is as if "you had all your hair shaved off like a convict, and now you tie a silver ribbon around this head without any hair. It just looks peculiar. . . . And look at them elbows. . . . Here you got on this grown woman's evening dress. . . . And that brown crust on your elbows. The two things just don't mix" (106–7). Through such absurd mimicry of femininity, overlaid with her tomboyishness, Frankie fails to rehearse a properly feminine gender role and so reveals the approximate nature of the process.

It is Frankie's play with nomenclature that emphatically signals her donning of femininity. As earlier noted, the fact that Frankie chooses, in her assumption of the F. Jasmine identity, such a highly feminine mask and exaggerates it serves to parody the very notion of a natural and original gender. As the "connected" and romantic F. Jasmine, Frankie dreams of a future where "Captain Jarvis Addams sinks twelve Jap battleships . . . [and] Mrs Janice Addams [is] elected Miss United Nations in beauty contest" (139). Now, for the first time, she listens intently to Berenice's rhetoric of love (119), and she "dressed carefully . . . in her most grown and best, the pink organdie, and put on lipstick and Sweet Serenade" (61) to go about town. As F. Jasmine, she entertains a "romance" with the soldier in the Blue Moon, which makes her feel "very proper. . . . [S]he carefully smoothed down her dress . . . so as not to sit the pleats out of the skirt" (84).

In choosing the orange satin evening dress for the wedding (106) and in wishing that she had "long bright yellow hair" (25), Frankie is undermining her attempts at femininity. It is a "not nice" dress as opposed to the "nice" pink organdie already hanging in her closet. By wishing for *bright*-colored hair and by preferring a gaudy dress over the more subtle and demure "good girl" dress, Frankie exaggerates "what woman wears," as does the drag queen, to make a mockery of what woman should be and "naturally" *is*, that is, feminine. Her clumsy attempts to become a woman underscore womanliness as performance.

At the end of *The Member of the Wedding*, after F. Jasmine's failed attempt to become a "we of me," Frankie assumes the name that embodies the installment of correct gender identification: "Frances," sensible Frances. She is "just mad about Michelangelo," reads Tennyson, and plans to become a poet herself, all acceptably feminine pursuits and ambitions. As Frances, she enters into an acceptable friendship with Mary Littlejohn. "[T]he daytime was now filled with radar, school, and Mary Littlejohn" (189), her dreams of boyish adventure now diluted to a sensible trip around the world with Mary. However, Frankie, like Mick, cannot quite carry off womanliness. She still dreams of becoming "the foremost authority on radar" (186), a typically male job at the time; her unconscious reference to two homoerotic poets—Michelangelo and Tennyson—undermines her attempt to conform to an acceptably heterosexual female identity.[24] Furthermore, as I have already suggested, the relationship between Frances and Mary Littlejohn may not merely be one of friendship.

Frankie's parade of feminine masks, signaled by her name changes as well as her dress, parodies any notion of a fixed identity. There is no such thing here as a peeling away of masks in the hope of getting to some firm core. Beneath each mask lies another, and another. The reader is foiled at every turn in any attempt to get to the bottom of identity through Frankie's various name-crossings, dress, and behavior. Behind the sensible "Frances" is the flighty "F. Jasmine," and behind her the tomboy "Frankie." But the masquerade does not stop there for "Frankie" is another mask, of masculinity, which enacts a type of gender suspension.

Like her younger counterparts, Miss Amelia Evans also appears from time to time as a woman. When the hunchback Cousin Lymon comes to town, love, the magic potion resembling her whiskey, which heightens sensitivities to the world around (*B* 15), feminizes Amelia. She opens up the café, which effects for the first time a strong community feeling in the town. She makes the store cheerful and bright (*B* 21–22) and decorates it with flowers (*B* 50). She becomes the perfect hostess, allowing the townsfolk to drink and eat in the store for the first time ever. In love, "her long brown face was somewhat brightened. . . . Her lips were not so firmly set as usual. . . . Her skin had paled" (*B* 29–30). Other changes take place: "During the week she still wore swamp boots and overalls, but on Sunday she put on a dark red dress. . . . Her manners . . . and her way of life were greatly changed. She still loved a fierce lawsuit, but she was not so quick to cheat her fellow man and to exact cruel payments" (*B* 31). Her new femininity also arises in her role of nurturer, of carer, in her relationship to Cousin Lymon, a relationship which, as suggested earlier, resembles that of mother and child.

However, I am finally left to wonder why McCullers's tomboys act like women at all. Their reason for acting like men was predicated on the offer or promise of comparable freedom through the disavowal of simple gender categories. It is more difficult to imagine why they might assume femininity. But to conceive gender as a choice is to misunderstand it. Thus, the young tomboys must submit, to some extent, to the societal pressures around them to conform to womanliness. However, because Mick and Frankie foreground the normative practices at work in creating gendered subjects, they resist being reduced to a mere image of woman. Once the masquerade of gender (in this case, femininity) is assumed deliberately, it reveals the gap between image and practice or experience. Masquerade enables the manipulation, with a vengeance, of the image of femininity and so becomes a mode of *empowerment* (Doane 87).

This dynamic is most clear in *The Ballad of the Sad Café*, where it is in the moments of feminine masquerade that Miss Amelia is at the height of her power. Amelia wears two examples of feminine garb—the wedding dress and the red dress—at the most crucial points of the text, when power is at stake: her marriage to Marvin Macy, the Sabbath, and the return of Marvin Macy.

In *Vested Interests*, Garber comments that "it is in the discussion of 'marriage' that the necessary questioning of the idea of the 'original' and the 'copy' has taken its most effective form." Noting the prevalence of transvestite mock "weddings," she concludes that "in a way all marriages, even heterosexual marriages are 'mock marriages,' in their dependence upon certain aspects of sartorial tradition and ceremony. . . . What gets married *is* a dress" (141, 142).

On the day of her marriage to Marvin Macy, Amelia "strode with great steps down the aisle . . . wearing her dead mother's bridal gown, which was of yellow satin and at least twelve inches too short for her. . . . As the marriage lines were read Miss Amelia kept making an odd gesture—she would rub the palm of her right hand down the side of her satin wedding gown. She was reaching for the pocket of her overalls, and being unable to find it, her face became impatient, bored, and exasperated. . . . They [the townsfolk] counted on the marriage . . . to change her at last into a calculable woman" (*B* 37–38). Amelia's utter discomfort and the strangeness of the dress emphasize Garber's point. The incongruity of the dress (of the whole event, in fact) underscores it as parodic performance. It is almost as if the masculine Amelia is cross-dressed, lending to the ceremony overtones of the transvestite mock wedding. (This episode also anticipates her wearing of the red dress, which reveals "a piece of her strong, hairy thigh" [*B* 71]). So, Amelia is only able to *approximate* her role as the beautiful bride, and in the process she unveils this ideal model of femininity as artifice. Even as she acts the demure and submissive bride, the good little woman, Amelia, consciously or unconsciously, overturns the norms of gendered identity.

The wedding represents (as all weddings in fact do) the domestication and heterosexualization of social relations. This is particularly apparent if the woman is a freak, a giant, associated with unruly nature, like the Amazon Amelia. However, Amelia's refusal, or perhaps inability, to conform to the ritual unsettles such normative discipline. Not only does she make a mockery of the wedding ceremony, but she also fails to consummate it, preferring to sit up with her father's pipe and *The Farmer's Almanac:* she is "ignorant of the message flashed to Marvin Macy by her . . . wedding gown" (Westling 177). Like Frankie who yearns to join her brother's wedding as a way of avoiding sex, Amelia sees no necessary connection between the ceremony and its consummation: in this respect she appears to be the instrument—albeit rather confused—of McCullers's subversive project.

Again, it is doubtful that Amelia is aware of the message sent to the world when "on Sunday she put on a dark red dress" (*B* 31), an effect of the feminizing influence of her love for Lymon. When Amelia chooses to parade the red dress, a symbol of feminine sexuality, it is on the holiest of days, the Sabbath. Amelia's flaunting has the same effect as Mick's graffiti, "PUSSY," written in big bold letters among such sacred names as that of Mozart. In these instances, both Mick and Amelia become Bakhtin's disobedient misreading fool. They combine elements that should never be combined; they misread the norms of appropriate association.

Further on in the narrative, "[f]or some reason, after the day of Marvin Macy's arrival, [Amelia] put aside her overalls and wore always the red dress" (*B* 64). It is "peculiar" and hangs "awkwardly around her bony knees" (*B* 68). That her dress is red has strong connotations of blood—particularly menstrual—and of fertility and sexual desire, as well as prostitution. Most readers claim that Amelia's dress on this occasion is, in one way or another, an acceptance of her "true" gender: "[T]he red dress signifies her femaleness within a context of her increasing loss of power" (Kahane, "Gothic Mirror" 348). However, a *red* dress would hardly do as a symbol of surrender. I would also reject suggestions that Amelia wears the dress to rekindle Marvin Macy's affection (Rechnitz 461); the text offers no suggestion whatsoever that it is Macy's attentions Amelia seeks. Furthermore, as Amelia demonstrates in her independent tomboy life, there are in fact other choices available. Finally, there is the proposition that the dress functions as a "symbol of her accessibility" (Broughton 41). But this makes no sense of Amelia's earlier refusal of sexual intercourse with Marvin Macy.

Westling offers a more plausible account. She believes that the red dress is "a flagrant reminder of [Marvin Macy's] failure to make her act the part of a woman during their marriage." Thus, the dress flaunts

Amelia's *inaccessibility:* "She will defy Marvin Macy even as she wears the clothing of a sex object he can never enjoy" (125, 177). It is as if, like Mick and Frankie, she turns her nose up at those who "counted on marriage . . . to change her at last into a calculable woman" (*B* 38) by, ironically, becoming what woman is expected to be. Miss Amelia and the tomboys take up the codes that oppress and capture them and use these very same codes as weapons against such absolute identity organization. In doing so, Miss Amelia and the tomboys make a mockery of heterosexual gender organization.

There is yet another form of power seemingly effected in Amelia's feminine masquerade, which resembles Biff's donning of female garb. In "Women on Top," Natalie Zemon Davis looks briefly at magical ritual transvestism: it "can be part of adolescent rites of passage" or "can ward off danger from demons [Marvin Macy?], malignant fairies [Cousin Lymon?] or other powers that threaten castration or defloration" (130). After Marvin Macy's return to town, the mannish Amelia, in her red dress, again seems to be cross-dressed as a woman and invokes the figure of the shaman,[25] just as Biff Brannon's feminine attire alludes to rituals of fertility. Along with her whiskey that reveals the secrets of the heart mentioned early on in the story, at this time, her witch-like powers seem to increase as "she began to take steps to clear up the situation": "she set a terrible trap for [Marvin Macy] out in the swamp. . . . [T]hen [she] tried to trip him up as he went down the steps" (*B* 64–65). "[O]n one occasion Miss Amelia tried to poison Marvin Macy" (*B* 68). Seven is her favorite number, and she relies on it for self-empowerment: "Her treatment nearly always hinged on this number. It is a number of mingled possibilities, and all who love mystery and charms set store by it. So the fight was to take place at seven o'clock" (*B* 77).

Since the donning of female garb is a symbol of access to divine knowledge and wisdom, suggestive of "the watchman of the night,"[26] this might mean that Amelia wears a dress at crisis points of the narrative to access power in the face of threat. However, as she prepares for the fight, the ultimate test of how far she may transgress, "Miss Amelia had changed her red dress for her old overalls" (*B* 78), perhaps in the hope that as in ancient "rituals of status reversal," dressed as a man, she might "turn aside an impending catastrophe" (N. Davis 130).

It becomes clear, then, that the females and males in question enact a "double displacement" (Spivak, "Displacement"), that is, the transvestites and cross-dressers, both male and female, masquerade *twice*. For, as I have shown, in McCullers's texts one's "original" gender appears as much a "doing" as the performing of the "other" gender. Spivak argues that such double displacement is more specifically the condition of woman, who experiences an "originary displacement" since she is already a "dissimulator" in a cultural discourse deemed "phallocentric." For woman to participate in such discourse (from which she is excluded as "woman") she must "impersonate"[27] once more, in order to "re-present" a place for herself (Spivak, "Displacement" 185). According to this interpretative framework, Miss Amelia and the young tomboys masquerade both a femininity and a partial masculinity. That this is most obvious in the women and not in the men in McCullers's texts has to do with the specularity of their own gender. By contrast, masculinity is the more difficult gender to parodically perform, and masculine gender appears as less displaced than feminine gender.

Although gender may not be a matter of choice, it is nevertheless mobile, contingent, and performative. In presenting gender as a ceaseless assumption of masks, McCullers's texts disrupt any notion of stable and originary gender. What emerges from an examination of female transvestism and male cross-dressing is a suspension (albeit temporary) of either/or gender categories. The enactment of one's *own* gender, ideally perceived as wholly appropriate and natural, is, ironically, as much a performance as crossing over to the other gender.

Substantiating gender processes seem to fail drastically in McCullers's works. None of her fictional creations is able to settle on *a* gender (let alone the right one), and in those brief moments in which they do, any notion of concrete identity is rapidly displaced. In this sense, all McCullers's gender freaks might be said to be grotesque since, in their excessiveness, they provide a challenge to any concept of a discretely finished, clearly gendered identity. The following chapter will engage more closely with this issue in a discussion of androgyny in *The Heart Is a Lonely Hunter* and *The Ballad of the Sad Café*.

4
Two Bodies in One
The Heart Is a Lonely Hunter and *The Ballad of the Sad Café*

Fundamental to this account of the grotesque in McCullers's texts is the anxiety attending the formation of identity. This anxiety takes the form of various tensions, which include those between the adolescent promise of lines of flight and social demands for conformity, between the male body and its feminization, and between femininity and masculinity. The Bakhtinian concept of "two bodies in one" (*Rabelais* 52) can elucidate what is occurring in such tensions.

Most immediately, "two bodies in one" conjures up the figure of androgyny. Although there are several characters whom we might consider androgynous, such as Singer, Mick, and Frankie, I will focus on a comparison between male androgyny, in the figure of Biff Brannon, and female androgyny, in the figure of Miss Amelia Evans, in terms of classical androgyny and what I term "grotesque androgyny" to reveal that androgyny predicated on classical notions of synthesis and wholeness cannot adequately account for the types of subjectivity McCullers's texts explore. Traditional concepts of androgyny rely on the assumption that masculinity and femininity have a fixed essence, whereas, as we have seen, McCullers conceives of gender in terms of masquerade. Not only is gender nomadic, but it is the tension *between* gendered subject possibilities that produces McCullers's grotesque subjects.

First, then, I trace more traditional readings of androgyny in both *The Heart Is a Lonely Hunter* and *The Ballad of the Sad Café*, highlighting their limitations. I then weigh up the efficacy or otherwise of the Bakhtinian model of "two bodies in one." This involves a close examination of the concept of hybridity and different accounts of it in relation to McCullers's texts, as well as the idea of "spanning" as set out in her poem "Father, Upon Thy Image We Are Spanned," with the aim of recovering the meaning of grotesque subjectivity in McCullers's writings as a whole.

CLASSICAL ANDROGYNY

Classical conceptions of androgyny derive from Aristophanes' account, in Plato's *Symposium* (59–61, 190b–191c), of an early people whom he calls hermaphroditic. Aristophanes's hermaphrodite is representative of the ideal state of man. This symmetrical figure was one of three sexes[1] and had "the characteristics of both male and female," "with two organs of generation." All three sexes independently formed "a rounded whole . . . complete circle," an aesthetic of unity also found in the ephebic statuary of classical antiquity. To curb the power of these "formidable" figures, Zeus decided "to cut each of them in two." Platonic androgyny, then, represents a utopia of genderless innocence, before the fall into male and female, masculine and feminine.

Platonic formulations of androgyny persist in twentieth-century psychoanalytical discourse. Freud makes use of Plato's myth in "The Sexual Aberrations" to reflect the role of the sexual instinct according to which human beings "are always striving to unite again in love" (46).[2] Twentieth-century writers influenced by Platonic notions include Woolf, who explores the "great" androgynous mind in *A Room of One's Own*.[3] The sight of a young man and woman climbing into a taxi prompts her to think of the "unity of the mind": "The normal and comfortable state of being is that when the two love in harmony together, spiritually cooperating. If one is a man, still the woman part of the brain must have effect; and a woman also must have intercourse with the man in her. . . . It is when fusion takes place that the mind is fully fertilized and uses all its faculties" (92).

In the latter part of the century, the classical/psychoanalytical conception of androgyny inflects Anglo-American feminism of the 1960s and 1970s, of which June Singer and Carolyn Heilbrun are particularly representative. Both draw on Jungian concepts of the feminine and the masculine to call for a "recognition" of the androgynous mind, which would provide the potential to liberate both men and women from an either/or pattern of "appropriate behavior" (see Singer; Heilbrun, *Toward a Recognition*). The concept drew much criticism in the 1980s for its indifference to specific female concerns.[4] Nearly a decade after the publication of *Toward a Recognition of Androgyny,* Heilbrun continued to refute criticism by claiming that androgyny "seeks to suggest that sex roles are societal constructs which ought to be abandoned." Although she does admit that androgyny is only "a necessary stopping place on the road to feminism" ("Androgyny" 265), her concept (and defense) of androgyny neglects two differently marked bodies.

Several readings of androgyny in McCullers's novels emerged in the 1980s. Writing in much the same vein as Singer and Heilbrun, these commentators view androgyny as a positive and productive concept of "wholeness." For example, the supposed androgyny of Biff Brannon in *The Heart Is a Lonely Hunter* is equated with "artistic awareness" (Taetzsch 192), and it seems that "only the androgyns are capable of attempting to escape the isolation of man" (Box 117). Significantly, when it comes to the question of Miss Amelia's androgyny, she is identified as "grotesque, freak, queer, . . . witch-wizzard [*sic*]" (Carlton 60), or as "hermaphroditic" (Kahane, "Gothic Mirror" 347), which is the "bad" reality of the androgynous ideal, for the hermaphrodite is a freak (Garber, *Vice Versa* 211, 214, 218). In the following comparative examination of Amelia and Biff, which focuses on the trope of pregnancy as it is evoked by androgyny, I reveal the dissymmetry[5] of such a universal ideal. That is to say, the androgynous woman and the androgynous man *mean* quite differently. To ignore this difference is to ignore the nomadism and tension of subjectivity in McCullers's writings.

Due to the discrepant identification of Amelia and Biff as androgynes in critical writings, we must first establish that both characters can in fact be designated androgynous if the same criteria are applied. Since Biff's femininity and Amelia's masculinity have been discussed at great length in previous chapters, it is sufficient merely to note here Biff's masculine traits and Amelia's feminine traits in order to establish their respective androgyny.

While Biff looks masculine—his body is hard and hairy—he also has a stereotypically rational masculine mind. In the outline of *The Heart Is a Lonely Hunter*, McCullers describes Biff as "nearly always coldly reflective. . . . He has a passion for detail. It is typical of him that he has a small room . . . devoted to a complete and neatly catalogued file of the daily evening newspaper dating back without a break for eighteen years" ("Author's Outline" 146).[6] Throughout the text of the novel itself are many references to Biff as a thinker (*H* 17, 111–12, 116, 118, 120, 190, 302). At times Biff seems obsessive, for example, in his almost fetishistic cataloging of the newspapers. At other times he reveals uncanny insight, as when he perceives Singer's function as a personal god for the four "friends." Biff wonders: "[W]hy did everyone persist in thinking the mute was exactly as they wanted him to be—when most likely it was all a very queer mistake?" (*H* 197).

Strongly opposed to this type of masculine mind is the feminine intuitive mind, represented by Miss Amelia's superstitious beliefs, for example, in numerology. Furthermore, although she refuses to treat "female complaints," Amelia is nonetheless a powerful healer and "there was no disease so terrible but she would undertake to cure it" (*H* 23). And, to note again, it could be argued that Miss Amelia's love for Lymon also "feminizes" her. So, Amelia does manifest feminine traits. Somehow, in the critical literature, Amelia's rejection of heterosexuality has become indicative of her flight from the feminine. According to this rather suspect logic, we could also charge Biff, who refuses the "male role," with "flight from the masculine," thus barring him from "true" androgynous status. Nevertheless, for the sake of argument, Biff Brannon is as androgynous as Miss Amelia. Both show traits of the "other" gender as well as their "own" respective gender in both their appearance and behavior. However, to reiterate, curiously enough, very rarely in the critical literature is Amelia referred to as "androgynous."[7] In the main, such a label is reserved for Biff Brannon.

There is one further trait Miss Amelia and Biff Brannon share: a strong maternal/paternal desire, which paradoxically eschews physical reproduction. The image of pregnancy is a fantasy evoked by the figure of androgyny. According to psychoanalytic theory, androgyny is equated "with a repressed desire to return to the imaginary wholeness and self-sufficiency associated with the pre-Oedipal phase before sexual difference" (Weil 3). That is to say, the fantasy of motherhood/fatherhood conjures up the image of a pre-Oedipal plenitude, which is associated with classical androgyny and involves the erasure of lapsarian sexual difference as, for instance, in Aristophanes's hermaphrodite. To focus on the trope of pregnancy in *The Heart Is a Lonely Hunter* and *The Ballad of the Sad Café* is to draw out once and for all the inherent dissymmetry or sexual indifference of classical androgynous wholeness.

Biff is "both maternal and paternal" (Phillips, "Gothic Architecture" 65): he sends whiskey to Doctor Copeland's son, Willie, while he is in prison; he treats his niece, Baby Wilson, as one of his own; he offers Jake Blount only kindness, both material and otherwise. Furthermore, Biff yearns to be both omnipotent mother and father at once, that is, to give birth without procreative sexuality. There is a part of Biff "that sometimes almost wished he was a mother and that Mick and Baby were his kids" (*H* 119). Lucile remarks that "'you'd make a good mother.' 'Thanks,' Biff said. 'That's a compliment'" (*H* 203). Not surprisingly, he yearns "[t]o adopt a couple of little children. A boy and a girl. About three or four years old so they would always feel like he was their own father. Their Dad. Our Father. . . . In the summer the three of them would go to a cottage on the Gulf. . . . And then they would bloom as he grew old. Our Father" (*H* 207). One reader concludes that Biff's "androgyny does not stand opposed either to women or to procreation." Instead, Biff will combine the two: "Biff dreams of nurturing, self-sacrificing, interactive responsibilities, not of fathering as opposed to mothering, but of parenting. Nor is parenting necessarily biological" (Budick 159). According to this view, Biff is the "pregnant man," equated with androgynous plenitude, for "the common representation of the hermaphrodite is that of a figure endowed with breasts and a penis; the female genitalia do not figure. . . . Seen in this light, the hermaphrodite appears less as a woman with a penis and more as a man with breasts." Significantly, the androgynous fantasy of the pregnant man allows the male access to "the powerful status he himself attributed to his mother" (Pacteau 74, 76). This scene is played out in *The Heart Is a Lonely Hunter* in Biff's relationship to his own mother, of whom he is in great awe: "She was a tall, strong woman with a sense of duty like a man. She had loved him best. Even now he sometimes dreamed of her. And her worn gold wedding ring stayed on his finger always" (199).

Similarly, Amelia has maternal yearnings that do not involve physical procreation. The text constructs her as "the phallic woman" of psychoanalytic theory, the female equivalent (which, I will argue, is in no way equivalent) of the pregnant man. Like the pregnant man, the phallic woman suggests a pre-Oedipal plenitude, representing "the child's fantasy of an omnipotent and absolutely powerful, sexually neutral figure" (Grosz, "Phallic Mother" 314). Just as Biff's relationship with his mother might explain his androgyny, so might Amelia's with her father. In *The Ballad of the Sad Café*, Amelia is raised alone by her father (20) who, after his death, "was . . . an interminable subject which was dear to her. . . . Miss Amelia never mentioned her father to anyone else except Cousin Lymon. That was one of the ways in which she showed her love for him" (45–46). Thus, her androgyny could stem from a desire to incorporate the power of the father, the phallus.

With no children of her own, Amazonian and sexually uninterested, Amelia, in her role of healer, behaves as a mother toward the sick children: she makes up special "gentler and sweeter" potions so that they might avoid the often violent effects of the powerful adult drugs (*B* 22). Mother-like, Amelia responds compassionately to Lymon's tears when he first arrives in town (*B* 14), and as her love develops, she comes to watch over him protectively: "There was a softness about her grey, queer eyes and she was smiling gently to herself. Occasionally she glanced from the hunchback to the other people in the café—and then her look was proud, and there was in it the hint of a threat, as though daring anyone to try to hold him to account for all his foolery" (*B* 50). "She spoiled him to a point beyond reason" (*B* 31), putting him to bed in the evenings, making sure that his prayers have been said before tucking him in (*B* 54). Lymon is for Amelia "a child acquired without pain" (Millichap, "Carson McCullers" 335), just as Mick Kelly and Baby Wilson are for Biff Brannon. It is fair to conclude, as the townsfolk do, that if Amelia and Lymon "had found some satisfaction between themselves, then it was a matter concerning them and God alone. All sensible people agreed in their opinion about this conjecture—and their answer was a plain, flat *no*" (*B* 32–33).

Biff's refrain, "Our Father" (*H* 207), cited earlier, epitomizes the pre-Oedipal plenitude already suggested by the maternal/paternal yearnings of the androgynous Amelia and Biff. He is the pregnant man, while she is the phallic woman. However, there is an obvious dissymmetry between the man and the woman who seek androgyny. Psychoanalytic theory, for example, does not consider (the fantasy of) the androgynous pregnant man a menacing figure. At worst, he represents "a descent into feminine castration and abjection." On the other hand, the fantasy of the phallic *woman*, in her "monstrous ascent into phallicism," is a powerful and unsettling figure in psychoanalytic discourse: "'[H]aving the phallus' is much more destructive as a feminine operation than as a masculine one, a claim that . . . implies that there is no other way for women to assume the phallus except in its most killing modalities" (Butler, *Bodies That Matter* 103).

Within the framework of the menacing fantasy of the phallic woman, it could be said that the phallic/uncastrated/masculine Miss Amelia becomes the castrator of Marvin Macy: she denies him the position of having the phallus in order to save her own phallic position. This bears out Butler's assertion that "[t]he failure to submit to castration appears capable of producing only its opposite, the spectral figure of the castrator. . . . The figure of excessive phallicism, typified by the phallic mother, is devouring and destructive, the negative fate of the phallus when attached to the feminine position" (*Bodies That Matter* 102). Amelia must therefore be punished as, in fact, she is.

As I noted in the preceding chapter, Amelia's more threatening status as the Amazonian phallic woman may lie in the fact that her masculinity, or androgyny, is manifested publicly, while Biff's androgyny occurs in private. Nevertheless, as readers, we of course have access to Biff's private feminine performance and yearnings, and it is in the responses of various McCullers commentators that the shortcomings of androgyny, in terms of its *indifference*, can be found.

In "The Flowering Dream," McCullers describes Amelia's maternal love for the hunchback dwarf as "strange" (287). Within *The Ballad of the Sad Café* itself, Amelia's rejection of sexual relations in favor of an asexual maternal love is viewed as an oddity. For example, when earlier Amelia weds Marvin Macy, the townsfolk, who had hoped that it would turn her into "a calculable woman," consider the fiasco of the unconsummated marriage "unholy" (38). The crucial element here is the condemnation heaped on Miss Amelia for her refusal to gather bride-fat, as well as for her later asexual, and so nonreproductive, relationship with a dwarf. The responses of the text's readers reflect such condemnation: Amelia is chastised for kicking out Marvin Macy (a mere "mischief-maker") and blamed for his subsequent life of crime (Roberts 94–95); Marvin Macy is, remember, no less than a rapist; or Amelia is censured for her rejection of heterosexuality.[8] These critics implicitly equate women's function with heterosexual reproduction. Amelia is therefore condemned, both inside and outside the ballad, for her rejection of "womanly" procreative duties, underscored by her "strange" maternal, nonsexual love for Cousin Lymon.

Conversely, Lucile (along with several commentators) deems it acceptable for Biff Brannon to indulge his maternal/paternal predilection toward both Mick Kelly and Baby Wilson, and to adopt children. Although Biff himself senses something "wrong" (*H* 25) in his unusual feelings, his odd desires are nevertheless left unchallenged while Amelia's are not.[9] There is no doubt, however, that Biff's feelings toward Mick are not merely those of a caring parent. There are definite sexual nuances in Biff's relationship with the young tomboy.[10] Barely able to speak to Mick (*H* 20, 109, 199), Biff blushes at the mere sight of her (*H* 186). On another occasion, "[h]e watched her as she stood behind the counter and he was troubled and sad. He wanted to reach out his hand and touch her sunburned, tousled hair—but not as he had ever touched a woman" (*H* 109).

L. Taetzsch asserts, rather cryptically, that Biff's feeling for Mick is "not the sexuality of a man toward a woman, but an androgyn toward an androgyn" (194). Certainly, Biff acknowledges that he would like to touch Mick as he never has a woman, but this in no way discounts other forms of pleasure and desire. (In any case, Taetzsch's argument could just as easily apply to Miss Amelia's affection for the seemingly sexless Cousin Lymon.) Biff censures himself to some extent for his strange desire for Mick: four weekends in a row, Biff "had walked in the neighborhood where he might see Mick. And there was something about it that was—not quite right. Yes. Wrong" (*H* 205). Biff's feeling of "tenderness" for Mick makes him "uneasy" (*H* 23, 109). "He had done nothing wrong but in him he felt a strange guilt. Why? The dark guilt of all men, unreckoned and without a name" (*H* 205). Perhaps this dark guilt refers to a fascination with the sexually undifferentiated prepubescent body. This would make sense of the fact that once Mick grows into womanhood, Biff feels "only a sort of gentleness. In him the old feeling was gone. For a year this love had blossomed strangely. He had questioned it a hundred times and found no answer" (*H* 311).

Furthermore, while rejection of heterosexual desire is a negative trait in Amelia, curiously, Biff's asexuality seems to be a mark of superior character. Budick, for example, hails "Biff's denial of his sexuality" as a sign that he is "not limited by biology." She goes on: "Biff will adopt . . . children, not produce them biologically. . . . Biff is not restricted by convention" (151, 159). For some reason, however, Miss Amelia is heavily delimited by cultural attitudes and constrictions. Her shunning of reproductive sexuality means only that she is a reprehensible, mannish freak.

In fact, Biff's impotence becomes a sign of the transcendence of the *drech*—the "intake and alimentation and reproduction" (*H* 204)—of human experience, to fulfill the dream of androgynous wholeness. Biff's impotence supposedly allows him to "embrace . . . a metamorphosis into a more enlightened entity," "into artistic, enlightened androgyny" (Taetzsch 192–93).[11] Thus, while Amelia is entwined in the equation woman/mother, Biff, the man, can transcend the body to be the androgynous Everyman, the universal transcendent subject, freed from the bodily constraints of sex. That Biff is impotent and thus genitally "distanced" only furthers these contrasting constructions of "man" and "woman": he can be representative of the "human," while Amelia, on the other hand, is caught in the boarded-up building, her body.

It is generally agreed that Alice Brannon, Biff's wife, plays an important role in his "developing androgyny." For example, along with his impotence, Alice's death enables Biff "to effect within himself a kind of marriage between the male and female, and his direct sexual needs are sublimated into parental emotions" (Roberts 83).[12] In some sense, Alice is killed off in the text so that Biff's developing androgyny can manifest itself. What is suggested here is male appropriation of the feminine, a problem that has great currency today when many male Continental philosophers espouse a kind of "becoming-woman" or a "feminine voice." We must ask in response, how does this affect real women? Reconsidered in this light, Biff's private (and for the most part unremarked-upon) appropriation of Alice's femininity subtly insinuates that he can perform femininity better than she ever could. Alice, the "real" woman, seems to be superfluous. So, Biff Brannon is not a fine model for the "recognition of androgyny" but, conceivably, the usurper of Alice's feminine subjectivity, of her experience as a woman. This clearly counters the claim, mentioned earlier, that "Biff's androgyny does not stand opposed . . . to women" (Budick 159).

Biff believes that Alice makes him "tough and small and as common as she was" (*H* 17). To lessen her defiling affects, the couple call each other "Mister and Misses [*sic*]" (*H* 17), they do not sleep together (*H* 32), and he will not undress in front of her (*H* 32). In sum, Biff is repulsed by "his good-looking plump wife" (*H* 56). It is Alice who apparently impedes Biff's developing androgyny and who has "forced" him "to superficially assume the male role. . . . After her death he takes a complete bath [*H* 112], an action which suggests his washing himself of the male role as well as his recognizing that he no longer needs to be physically repugnant. He then becomes more androgynous, feeling no necessity to hide his sensitivity by conforming to a static sex role" (Box 122).[13] Again, it is as if Biff can transcend the *drech* of human being. Oddly, in this reading, it is *masculinity* that appears to be the muddying gender, something of which Biff needs to be cleansed before he can assume Alice's femininity. More commonly, it is femininity, the female body, that is aligned with the abject.

Because Alice impedes Biff's androgyny, she must be annulled. The text therefore kills her off, for it is what she *represents,* that is, femininity, that is of real significance for the man seeking androgyny. And once she dies, Biff cannot remember anything about her, except for "her feet—stumpy, very soft and white and with puffy little toes" (*H* 117).[14] In a similar way, Biff feels that the only way to deal with Alice when she is alive is with silence (*H* 17). He has, in a sense, usurped her and colonized the very memory of her. Thus, within the dynamic of appropriation, it is absence that marks "real" women, and what is emphasized is the death of the other; in this case, it is a literal death.

The Heart Is a Lonely Hunter constructs Alice's femininity quite differently from the femininity Biff later appropriates. While Alice is alive, Biff considers her a petty nagger (120). Yet once Biff takes on Alice's apparently annoying idiosyncrasies, he transforms them into an androgynous ideal. According to the logic of appropriation, it makes sense, then, that it is *after* Alice's death that Biff begins to yearn to adopt children (207). By improving on Alice's own feminine traits, rendered stereotypical in her, Biff is able to incorporate them into his (male) self to become the omnipotent maternal/paternal "Our Father." Biff ponders this dynamic himself when, buffing his nails as Alice buffed hers (56) and using her Agua Florida and lemon hair rinse, he wonders: "Certain whims that he had ridiculed in Alice were now his own. Why?" (198). And again: "[T]he one who has gone is not really dead, but grows and is created for a second time in the soul of the living" (111).[15] This analysis makes apparent a rather sinister implication of male androgyny: through Biff's appropriation of Alice's seemingly second-rate femininity, he is better able to control and then to rearticulate the feminine according to his own (male) terms, separating the feminine from the experience of "real" female subjectivity at the same time. By denigrating Alice's womanliness and subsequently appropriating it, Biff makes Alice the ground to his figure, to his androgynous self-representation.

In his appropriation of the feminine, Biff Brannon is reminiscent of Ovid's Tiresias, who is empowered by his foray into femininity to return a better man (67). Biff Brannon, too, becomes a seer as he accesses, even if briefly, "a glimpse of human struggle and of valour," as one eye "delved narrowly into the past" and the other "gazed wide and affrighted into a future of blackness, error, and ruin" (*H* 312). While we might associate the androgynous Biff with the seer, a shaman-like figure,[16] significantly, when it comes to the question of Miss Amelia's legendary powers, she is labeled a witch.[17] Unlike Biff, she is never accorded shamanistic status. Furthermore, again like Tiresias, Biff returns a man—"But, motherogod, was he a sensible man or not?" (*H* 312). Biff's story is "the safe story of the recovery of reason" (Spivak, "Three Feminist Readings" 24).

I have shown that the concept of classical androgyny is primarily a male aspiration and a male achievement. It is also potentially a misogynistic image: first, in its denial of any true androgyny for the woman who becomes instead a dangerous freak, unrepresentative of the Platonic ideal, and second, insofar as the male subject colonizes femininity, which he then performs in a superior fashion. I would agree with the assertion, then, that androgyny "rests on the assumption that the kind of body we have puts no limits on the personalities we might develop; this is really just like Plato's assumption that any kind of soul or mind can exist in our bodies" (Spelman 124). A static model such as classical androgyny ignores the many tensions in McCullers's fictional worlds.

GROTESQUE ANDROGYNY

Given the inadequacy of the classical model, the type of androgyny Bakhtin describes in *Rabelais and His World* is a more useful model with which to illuminate the irresolvable tensions of identity in McCullers's texts. Although also concerned with the notion of "two in one," grotesque androgyny is open-ended and always in process, not a completed whole. No synthesis takes place; the "two in one" is, literally, the image of the unfinished.

Like the classical model, however, Bakhtin's configuration of grotesque androgyny seems to appropriate the feminine. Bakhtin's "two bodies in one" does not merely invoke the fantasy of pregnancy as classical androgyny does; it explicitly uses images of the pregnant body as its basis. To recall, the grotesque rests on the image of the pregnant body. Bearing in mind that the Bakhtinian carnival world is open to men alone (*Rabelais* 13), the image of the pregnant "two bodies in one" recalls the "pregnant man" of androgynous plenitude. Thus, as with the classical model of androgyny, women once more risk becoming the ground for male carnivalesque subjectivity.

Bakhtin's focus on the "material bodily lower stratum," which gives birth to carnivalesque subjectivity, invokes the image of the pregnant body time and time again: "This is the pregnant and begetting body, or at least a body ready for conception and fertilization, the stress being laid on the phallus or the genital organs. From one body a new body always emerges in some form or other" (*Rabelais* 26).[18] Intertwined with such images of birth and pregnancy are those of death, for death is part of the process of renewal: "To degrade is to bury, to sow, and to kill simultaneously, in order to bring forth something *more and better.* To degrade also means to concern oneself with the lower stratum of the body. . . . Degradation digs a bodily grave for a new birth; it has not only a destructive, negative aspect, but also a regenerating one" (*Rabelais* 21, emphasis added).[19] This suggests once more the death, or at least the absence, of the other, which leads to the birth of the new subject. Just as Biff emerges a "more and better" person after Alice's death, as he appropriates her feminine vitality, the new body of which Bakhtin conceives, also born from death, is a "more and better" body. In a dynamic congruent to the relationship between Alice and Biff, the grotesque body, with its conjoined images of birth and death, enacts a "caesarian operation [which] kills the mother but delivers the child" (*Rabelais* 206). This image recalls Alice's death from "a tumour almost the size of a newborn child" in *The Heart Is a Lonely Hunter* (110).[20]

It can be argued, then, that misuse or appropriation of the feminine for the creation of a new identity occurs throughout *Rabelais and His World*. For example, woman is "first of all . . . the *principle* that gives birth. She is the womb" (240, emphasis added).[21] As mentioned, it is the male subject, the new man, to which she gives birth. In *The Ballad of the Sad Café*, for example, the androgynous Amelia is defeated in giving birth to a new form of subjectivity for herself. Like Alice, she is killed off, made absent, to allow for the birth of the alliance between Marvin Macy and Cousin Lymon. Thus, once more, woman's experience becomes superfluous as the *idea* of the feminine is rent from her reality. It is frequently argued that at the same time that women are excluded from carnivalesque subjectivity, they are also "the *other* that enables the perspective of the free and open-ended (male) *I*" (Ginsburg 167). These charges are reminiscent of those made against classical androgyny.

There is another element of Bakhtin's delineation of androgyny that several feminist commentators find problematic. This is that the maternal, the female, and the grotesque become equated with one another (Ginsburg 166, 170).[22] In *Rabelais and His World*, there is no alternative model of feminine subjectivity to the maternal grotesque. So, woman is caught within the strictures of reproductive functions. There are, however, several ways in which McCullers's texts engage with the problems resulting from Bakhtin's grave/womb image, that is, the problems of male appropriation of the feminine and of the alignment of the female with the grotesque and maternal body.

To re-address the issue of feminine appropriation in *The Heart Is a Lonely Hunter*, it is worthwhile to look closely at the effects that a newly acquired femininity has on Biff Brannon. Counter to what many believe, namely, that he is enriched and enlightened by his androgyny, Biff's femininity is, rather, symbolic of his decline. In a sense, it is as if femininity avenges itself. The feminine here is not "pregnant" but disempowering and debilitating. I have repeatedly cited the subversive influence of femininity or the feminine in McCullers's fiction: as the unruly and spectacular body of the adolescent girls; as an unmanning force on the ideal male body; and as a parodic dynamic in the hyperbolically feminine women. Although the lack of adult women and their voices constitutes a major gap in McCullers's texts, when the feminine comes to work on different bodies, it becomes a powerful force. The femininity Biff acquires from Alice is no exception.

By mapping onto Biff's androgyny this conceptualization of femininity and woman as it occurs in McCullers's texts, we quickly realize that Biff's increasing androgyny actually signals his impotence as he performs "like a woman," that is, as a castrated man. After Alice's death, Biff begins to feel old, although he is only forty-four (*H* 205, 209), and "the business was losing money. There were many slack hours" (*H* 199). Caught up in a crippling nostalgia (*H* 120, 199, 208), "uneasy" and "afraid" (*H* 311), he is left with no one person to love, "leaving him either better or worse. Which? However you looked at it" (*H* 310). McCullers herself discusses the association of Biff's enervation with his femininity in her "Author's Outline of 'The Mute'": "at forty-four years [Biff] is prematurely impotent," and "as a compensation for his own dilemma," he believes that "human beings are fundamentally ambi-sexual—and for confirmation he turns to the periods of childhood and senility" (146). McCullers adds that Biff's acquisition of his dead wife's habits is "a reflection of his own feeling for his approaching decline and death" (148).

In *The Heart Is a Lonely Hunter,* Biff concludes that "by nature all people are of both sexes. . . . The proof? Because old men's voices grow high and reedy and they take on a mincing walk. And old women sometimes grow fat and their voices get rough and deep and they grow dark little moustaches. And he even proved it himself—the part of him that sometimes almost wished he was a mother" (119). Thus, his growing femininity is contiguous with the unmanning effects of old age and impotence. That this is the case undermines the many accounts that point to Biff's dream of wholeness, that is, the androgynous ideal. At the very end of *The Heart Is a Lonely Hunter,* Biff rejects his status as the "androgynous" seer to became once more a "sensible man."

The dynamic in androgyny, of a femininity that castrates the male, is also apparent in Ovid's story of Hermaphroditus in *Metamorphoses.* Seduced by the nymph, Salmacis, Hermaphroditus becomes two bodies in one: he "saw that the water had made him half a man, / With limbs all softness . . . a voice whose tone was almost treble" (93). Unlike the hermaphrodite of *Symposium,* in Ovid's story there is no sense of completion and wholeness. Hermaphroditus is indicative of the fallen state of man who is "contaminated" by female desire/Salmacis, not the utopian model Aristophanes' hermaphrodite signifies. Femininity in *The Heart Is a Lonely Hunter* has a similar overpowering force.

It is not just the male androgyne whose debility coincides with femininity. Amelia Evans, at the end of her story, is defeated by the conventions of a society that demands she become the personification of the principle of woman. As Westling notes, after Amelia's defeat in the fight, "it is the unmistakable body of a woman we see lying on the floor of the cafe" (177). Amelia "lay sprawled on the floor, arms flung outwards and motionless. . . . Someone poured water on Miss Amelia, and after a time she got up slowly and dragged herself into her office . . . she was sobbing with the last of her grating, winded breath. . . . Once she gathered her right fist together and knocked it three times on the top of her office desk, then her hand opened feebly and lay palm upward and still" (*B* 80–81). Cousin Lymon skips town with Marvin Macy. Amelia waits for him for three years, and "in the fourth year . . . Miss Amelia hired a Cheehaw carpenter and had him board up the premises, and there in those closed rooms she has remained ever since" (*B* 83). Amelia's potential for a true androgynous subjectivity is immured in the house, just as Biff turns away from his double vision to greet the morning. She becomes "unmanned": she lets her hair grow, her muscles shrink "until she was as thin as old maids. . . . Her voice was broken, soft, and sad as the wheezy whine of the church pump organ" (*B* 83), recalling the decline of Ovid's Hermaphroditus.[23]

That femininity has a castrating affect on the androgynous Miss Amelia and Biff Brannon underscores the observation that because "the woman's body stands for the signifier of lack, it follows that the [male] androgyne figure invariably evokes castration" (Pacteau 70). In the end, Biff comes closer to T. S. Eliot's Tiresias, an "old man with wrinkled dugs" (72),[24] because plenitude, as suggested by Biff's "Our Father," is problematically entangled with androgynous impotence. Thus, while Bakhtin's grotesque androgyny has birth arising from death, the fantasy of androgyny Biff Brannon enacts is, rather, "a narcissistic 'caress' in which the subject annihilates itself" (Pacteau 82), recalling the scene in *The Heart Is a Lonely Hunter* I discussed in the previous chapter where Biff stands before the mirror, gazing on his feminine self. The self-sufficient narcissism of the androgyne cannot be generative; beneath the omnipotence of the pregnant body is the threat of sterility, impotence. This is the descent into feminine castration that is the fate of the feminized man.

Another way in which *The Heart Is a Lonely Hunter* troubles the configuration of androgyny set out in *Rabelais and His World* and linked to the sterility of femininity is in its use of the tropes of ascent and descent. In his account of grotesque androgyny, Bakhtin insists on the centrality as well as the necessity of the role of the "material bodily lower stratum" (370), the location of genitals, bowels, womb, uterus, and thus creation: "To degrade . . . means to concern oneself with the lower stratum of the body, the life of the belly and the reproductive organs; it therefore relates to acts of defecation and copulation, conception, pregnancy, and birth" (21). Ginsburg finds this movement problematic in that, like Ovid's Tiresias, "[t]he grotesque carnival body is degraded into the 'lower bodily stratum' associated with the feminine, and, in the same breath, is elevated into a principle of universal significance as the Material Body, no longer that of woman" (167). On the other hand, Bakhtin's image of feminine degradation to produce carnivalesque subjectivity could instead pose "a challenge to male transcendence through the generative power of female immanence" (Cullingford 21). However, in *The Heart Is a Lonely Hunter*, the movement of the male toward femininity is *upward*, not downward. That is to say, Biff Brannon *transcends* the bodily functions. As already noted, Biff "was scrupulously clean from the belt upwards. Every morning he soaped his chest and arms and neck and feet—and about twice during the season he got into the bathtub and cleaned all of his parts" (32). Biff is repulsed by or fearful of "the material bodily lower stratum"; it is not the fruitful resource Bakhtin claims is the pivot of the grotesque body.

Finally, *The Ballad of the Sad Café* directly takes issue with, to undermine, the equation grotesque-maternal-female. Miss Amelia Evans is unable to be contained within these terms and so unsettles any literal alignment of female body with maternal body. Amelia is a grotesque, not merely because she is a woman but because she is both like a man and *un*reproductive. In other words, her grotesqueness does not emanate from an unruly female pregnant body. One reader goes so far as to assert that Amelia is a literal *phallic* figure: that she is "ugly, oversized, . . . elongated and masculine, suggests of course the phallus."[25] Although, as I have said, Amelia's rejection of her procreative duties is usually considered a major shortcoming, Russo astutely notes that "the distinction . . . between the mother's body and the female body is absolutely crucial to feminist cultural criticism and reproductive politics" (119). The distinction opens up alternative possibilities for female subjectivity outside culturally perceived and required roles for, and functions of, women. In a similar way, the prepubescent girls along with the numerous childless adult women throughout McCullers's texts offer other good examples of the jamming of the female-maternal-grotesque equation.[26] The burden of the equation is thus replaced with a possibility that women, too, can participate in an open-ended form of subjectivity and need not merely function as the ground to man's representation. McCullers has created a new grotesque: Amelia's androgyny means that she is in excess of any exclusive gendered subjectivity, yet in her "barrenness" she suggests a lack of what it takes to be a woman. She both exceeds and falls short.

McCullers's texts produce new forms of grotesque subjectivity that hinge on contradiction, a type of subjectivity the figure of androgyny cannot contain. Having said this, however, it is worth noting once more the vigor with which several feminist commentators on McCullers's work reject the label "grotesque" when it is attached to Amelia. However, there *is* potential in reading McCullers's texts in terms of Bakhtin's concept of the grotesque. For example, as we have seen, McCullers's portraits of Biff and Miss Amelia might counter feminist anxiety vis-à-vis the appropriation of the feminine implied by Bakhtin's grotesque. The worry is, first, that women are excluded from carnivalesque subjectivity yet simultaneously provide the ground for the new male, and second, that the grotesque becomes too easily equated with both the maternal and female. To try and avoid the possible risks of feminine appropriation some feminists find located in the grotesque, it is useful to explore Bakhtin's rhetorical device of hybridization. This notion of hybridity more satisfactorily describes the friction of the "two in one" in McCullers's texts than does the hazardous trope of pregnancy.

Hybridity emerges from Bakhtin's discussion of dialogism in his essay "Discourse in the Novel." Strictly speaking, hybridity, according to Caryl Emerson and Michael Holquist, involves "[t]he mixing, within a single concrete utterance, of two or more different linguistic consciousnesses, often widely separated in time and social space. . . . [T]heir double-voicedness is not meant to resolve" (*Dialogic Imagination* 429).[27] Elizabeth Cullingford draws out from this the idea that "hybridization or the mixing of messages corresponds . . . with a 'deconstructed' feminism, which undoes the binary oppositions of 'masculine' and 'feminine' in order to unsettle patriarchal prescriptions for gender identity" (26). Accordingly, gender identity is constantly being reviewed and reformed; hybridity produces not unity but "incompleteness, becoming, ambiguity, indefinability, non-canonicalism" (Clark and Holquist 312). It is, in fine, strictly antithetical to androgynous synthesis. Although the double-voiced hybrid is primarily a rhetorical device, its characteristics connote those of the grotesque in *Rabelais and His World:* "The essence of the grotesque is precisely to present a contradictory and double-faced fullness of life" (62). McCullers has a similar concept of the grotesquery of existence, which she defines as "the juxtaposition of the tragic with the humorous, the immense with the trivial, the sacred with the bawdy, the whole soul of man with a materialistic detail" ("Russian Realists" 258).

In *Rabelais and His World*, the hybrid appears in Rabelais's image of the hermaphrodite: "a man's body with two heads facing one another, four arms, four feet, a pair of arses and a brace of sexual organs, male and female" (323). Although Bakhtin calls this an image of androgyny, it is not concerned with synthesis, like classical androgyny, but with juxtaposition. A brief exploration of hermaphroditism illuminates both Bakhtin's concept of a hybrid "two bodies in one" and McCullers's world of irresolvable paradoxes. The hermaphrodite embodies an unstable and dynamic movement between two supposedly exclusive poles, male and female, thus differing from the androgyne, which seeks to smooth over (gender) difference in the name of the One.

Garber, pondering Jungian androgyny, concludes that there are "two kinds of androgyny, the good kind which was spiritual, mythical, 'archetypal,' and productive of intrapsychic oneness, and the bad kind, which was physical, sexy, and disturbing" (*Vice Versa* 211).[28] For, while the androgynous figure is a fantasy (it *seems* both male and female), the hermaphrodite *is* both, and so is a reality. In other words, the hermaphrodite is the "real" representation of "the impossible referent," the androgyne. Consequently, the hermaphrodite, with its "brace of sexual organs," is a freak, a grotesque; not a classical ideal, but an imperfect figure.

Kari Weil further clarifies the difference between static androgyny and truly grotesque hermaphroditism by drawing on Barthes's concepts of "paradoxism" and "antithesis."[29] She equates androgyny with antithesis, which is "a figure of stable opposition," a union of two halves. Hermaphroditism is closer to paradoxism, a hybrid figure of confusion that embodies "a more dynamic and unstable conflict." In the domain of gender, paradoxism, or hermaphroditism, is "created out of excess and the surpassing of boundaries" (35) and so "reveals both the instabilities of boundaries between categories of opposition such as masculine and feminine, and the self-serving function of their illusory symmetry" (12). Thus, like the hybrid, the hermaphrodite brings together, but not synthetically, elements usually kept ontologically separate. A true grotesque, the gender hybrid does not erase difference in the name of an androgynous synthesis. Instead, hybridity, like hermaphroditism, engages with—specifically sexual—difference, that is, it presents both genders at the same time, with the incessant jarring of a true paradoxism.

The figure of the hermaphrodite makes a brief appearance in *The Member of the Wedding.* Frankie and her cousin John Henry see "the Half-Man Half-Woman, a morphidite and a miracle of science" (27), on display in the Freak House. O'Connor also writes of the freak show hermaphrodite in "A Temple of the Holy Ghost." In both writers' texts, as I have already noted, the hermaphrodite becomes a symbol of the young girls' horror at the changing pubescent body.[30] However, perhaps even more powerfully, the hermaphrodite enacts a dynamic form of subjectivity.

The freak of "A Temple of the Holy Ghost" tells its audience that "God made me this way. . . . I never done it to myself nor had a thing to do with it" (97). This might suggest, symbolically, that gendered identity is not an option but a constant pull between different subject positions. The point is that a tense, or disrupted, identity is a condition of being human in McCullers's work.

Although the real figure of the hermaphrodite does not feature outside of the freak show, and only then in one novel, its effects of unstable juxtaposition nevertheless do haunt McCullers's writings. The most obvious image might be John Henry's hermaphroditic vision of the perfect world where everyone would be "half boy and half girl" (M 116), or again, Biff Brannon's belief that "by nature all people are of both sexes" (*H* 119). However, in the former, the image is the androgynous one whereby two complementary halves make up a whole; the latter evokes the fantasy, or psychic model, of androgyny as found, for instance, in Woolf's *A Room of One's Own*.

Rather, the notion of the "two in one," in which difference is maintained, occurs in McCullers's poem "Father, Upon Thy Image We Are Spanned": "Why are we split upon our double nature, how are we planned? / Father, upon what image are we spanned?. . . . Who said *it is finished* when Thy synthesis was just begun." McCullers imagines human being as split and, more pertinently, as unfinished; synthesis is impeded, so that androgyny is imperfect. The imperfect or ruptured unity allows for the viable tensions and shifts in identity set out in McCullers's texts.

The poem's notion of spanning, precluding any possibility of integration, further suggests the unfinished nature of human identity. Spanning suggests not a blending but rather *a two at once,* evidenced further by the unfinished nature of God's human creation. In *Gyn/Ecology,* Mary Daly develops her own concept of spanning. A productive concept, spanning breaks "mind-numbing combinations" of which androgyny, the blending of two complementary halves, is her example. "Spanning splits," she continues, "involves something Other than attempting to fasten together two apparently opposite parts, on the mistaken assumption that these 'halves' will make a whole" (386, 387).[31] In a similar way, "Father, Upon Thy Image We Are Spanned" articulates not an androgynous synthesis but a state of incompletion in the spirit of a hybrid hermaphroditism.

There are moments in *The Heart Is a Lonely Hunter* and *The Ballad of the Sad Café* in which spanning occurs in the realm of gender, either on the body's surface as clothing or in behavior. This is not androgyny, in which masculinity and femininity wholly merge to ignore sexual differentiation in order to achieve a static "roundness of being." It is, rather, a carnivalesque process in which supposedly contradictory elements are juxtaposed in the one body, in the form of the double-voiced hybrid.

Accordingly, in McCullers's texts, the dynamic of "two bodies in one" reveals that masculine and feminine are neither mutually exclusive nor potentially synthetic. Masculinity and femininity are in a constant state of agitation in her work. In *The Member of the Wedding* this is epitomized in the visiting cards Frankie makes one evening with "*Miss* F. *Jasmine Addams, Esq.*, engraved with squinted letters" (61, emphasis added). There is no merging of the heterodox elements, masculine naming and feminine naming. Rather, there is an unsettled and unsettling "two" at odds. There is a similar conflict in Mick's attempts to perform "as a woman" toward the end of *The Heart Is a Lonely Hunter*. Unlike Frankie, Mick does not change her name to reflect her newly acquired "womanliness" and thus, like Frankie's visiting cards, confounds masculinity and femininity in terms of nomenclature. Another example of gender hybridity occurs in *The Member of the Wedding* when Berenice comments on Frankie's incongruous appearance in the gaudy orange satin dress she chooses to wear to her brother's wedding. The dress does not mix with her boy's haircut and her dirt-encrusted elbows (106–7). In this sense, the hybrid image once more conjures up the figure of the fool of carnival. As noted in the previous chapter, I deemed the tomboys "foolish" in their inability to carry out "proper" gender performance, that is, the appropriate mask slipped to reveal something else. In the previous examples of hybridity, the young girls are again analogous to the fool who misreads the norms of appropriate association, who mixes messages.

The hybrid as fool appears again in *The Heart Is a Lonely Hunter* when Biff Brannon puts the dead Alice's "perfume on his dark hairy armpits" (198). Heterodox elements are brought disturbingly into play, but not in any complementary or symmetrical sense. Similarly, on the day of Miss Amelia's marriage to Marvin Macy, dressed in her mother's wedding gown, Amelia fumbles for the pocket of her overalls, in search of pipe and tobacco. Amelia also mixes messages when she wears her red dress on the Sabbath (*B* 31).

On another occasion, again in her red dress, Amelia warms herself by the stove: "She did not warm her backside modestly, lifting her skirt only an inch or two, as do most women when in public. There was not a grain of modesty about Miss Amelia. . . . Now as she stood warming herself, her red dress was pulled up quite high in the back so that a piece of her strong, hairy thigh could be seen" (*B* 71). The reader is forced to pause before this image of Amelia; she seems to be both man and woman. This is a perfect example of hybridity that defies the limits of the discretely gendered classical body to displace stable gender formation in terms of either/or. This occurs not in terms of an excluded half seeking wholeness, but more broadly in the juxtaposition of elements usually deemed mutually exclusive. Thus, what the hybrid moment neatly describes is the tension of grotesque subjectivity in McCullers's works and so points to the failure or impossibility of any stable identity.

The hybrid then, by its nature, is a figure of unsustainable dis-ease. Proof of this uneasiness lies in the fact that in the case of the young tomboys, southern society will not tolerate their waywardness and instead requires that they submit to cultural demands for "womanliness." Biff Brannon returns to the daylight world of sober reason, "a sensible man." Amelia is confined to the boarded-up café. Similarly, some critics have sought to contain the energy of the hybrid "two in one" in the static figure of androgyny because it is a more manageable synthesis of masculine and feminine.[32] So, for example, because Amelia cannot easily be positioned within the taxonomic bounds of classical androgyny, she is usually dismissed as a freak in her disavowal of her womanly functions.

The grotesque image of the hybrid best illuminates the dynamics of juxtaposition that underpin all of McCullers's writings. McCullers herself writes that "[p]aradox is a clue to communication, for what is *not* often leads to the awareness of what *is*" ("Flowering Dream" 284).[33] Even if instances of hybridity are only momentary, they nevertheless fruitfully account for the unfinished beings in McCullers's novels. More than this, the hybrid opens up the possibility of new lines of flight, not in terms of escape or transcendence of the human, which classical androgyny promises, but in terms of the transformation of how the human is understood. This is the principle that has informed my rereading of McCullers throughout, arguing that a rich conceptualization of the grotesque lies at the heart of McCullers's exploration of the strangeness of being alive.

Conclusion

Final Thoughts on the Grotesque

Carson McCullers's freakish fictional world, a world populated by dwarfs and giants, mutes, sexual deviants, and androgynes, is ripe for an analysis of the grotesque that privileges abnormality—the distorted body and its aberrant pleasures—over the pure-cut lines of the normal body. Although McCullers's grotesque subjects are painfully marginalized according to social and cultural norms, they mischievously disrupt the simple and fragile distinction between normal and abnormal, queer and straight. Although I have explored McCullers's grotesque world in the context of desire and gender in particular, there are, of course, other important elements that structure identity in her texts: race, class, disability, and age. A future focus on these elements, which overlap with sexuality and gender, might not only consolidate the status of McCullers's work as important social commentary but also point the way to further readings of McCullers's unfinished subjects.[1]

Throughout this study I have intermittently attended to the *pain* of the unfinished. The portrait of Honey Camden Brown in *The Member of the Wedding* epitomizes such pain as does Penderton's questioning of Langdon's wisdom in *Reflections in a Golden Eye*: "'You mean . . . it is better . . . for the square peg to keep scraping about the round hole rather than to discover and use the unorthodox square that would fit it . . . ?'" (*R* 112). The women in the novels—Miss Amelia, Mick, and Frankie—similarly experience the pain of compromised promise at the end of their respective stories. Even Biff, whose schizophrenic vision at the end of *The*

Heart Is a Lonely Hunter offers hope, experiences instead "a shaft of terror" (312). This element of pain finally needs addressing.

In the introduction I argued that more usual readings of the grotesque (or gothic) that focus on despair are inadequate in comprehensively accounting for the grotesquerie of McCullers's fiction. I set out to show the positive dynamics of her work using an alternative theory of the grotesque: Bakhtin's. However, McCullers's novels are hardly Rabelaisian texts of joyful ribaldry. While the Bakhtinian grotesque "liberates the world from all that is dark and terrifying[,] it takes away all fears and is therefore completely gay and bright" (*Rabelais* 47), McCullers's grotesque world is often hazardous, as it relays "the painful substance of life" ("Russian Realists" 263).

How, then, can we reconcile the differences of tenor between McCullers's texts and Bakhtin's Rabelais? It is important to return to McCullers's essay on realism in which she writes, "Life, death, the experiences of the spirit, these come and go and we do not know for what reason; but the *thing* is there, it remains to plague or comfort, and its value is immutable" ("Russian Realists" 260). This "thing" is the foundation of McCullers's ontological understanding: "the grotesque is paralleled with the sublime" ("Flowering Dream" 287). This is where the similarity between McCullers's and Bakhtin's conceptualizations of the grotesque lies and where we find the "some good" of McCullers's vision.

In "The Flowering Dream," McCullers observes that "writing, in essence, is communication; and communication is the only access to love. . . . For myself, the further I go into my work and the more I read of those I love, the more aware I am of the dream and the logic of God, which indeed is a Divine collusion" (287). McCullers's "Divine collusion" bears some relation to O'Connor's discussion of the southern grotesque: "[T]he characters have an inner coherence, if not always a coherence to their social framework. Their fictional patterns lean away from typical social patterns, toward mystery and the unexpected" (*Mystery and Manners* 40). What McCullers and O'Connor emphasize are the elements of sympathy and "coherence." McCullers's work is fascinating because of her empathy with her characters. Whereas in O'Connor's fiction the grotesques are a part of a pointedly satirical world, McCullers extends to her characters and their worlds understanding and, as she says herself, "love." Perhaps her own status as a social outsider enabled the profound compassion that underlies all her texts and allows her to acknowledge the pain of the unfinished, "the unexpected."

In McCullers's ontological conception, there is a coherence of a type O'Connor describes. This coherence obtains in the grotesque form of juxtaposition between birth and death, the two sides of life of which Bakhtin writes. McCullers's conceptualization of human being is analogous to the technique of "flickering" in which two alternative meanings exist and struggle in the same sphere, the same subject.[2] Her grotesques suffer from social oppression and marginalization, and endure the punishment meted out to those who do not perform appropriately. Yet, grotesque figures can also function as an incisive critique of the society that outlaws them.

The grotesque in McCullers's texts, then, has to do with *possibility* as it makes strange the category "human," which readers, in turn, are forced to reexamine. McCullers provides a portrait of human activity considered as an unfolding of possibility, even if at times such a process may be painful and subject to compromise. It is this which is at the heart of McCullers's grotesque portraits.

Critical Survey

McCullers and the Southern Grotesque

To date, there are three discernible strands in the critical appraisal of McCullers's work that have as their respective foci the adolescent, spiritual alienation, and the concerns and identity of women. All three approaches have connections with the grotesque: the adolescent is often read as a grotesque figure; spiritual alienation is symbolically represented by the grotesques; and finally, most feminist commentary has concentrated on the construction of women as grotesque. The grotesque has for a long time defined the literature of the South. William Van O'Connor, for example, claims that "[p]erhaps the South has produced more than its share of the grotesque . . . : Erskine Caldwell, William Faulkner, Robert Penn Warren, Eudora Welty, Carson McCullers, Flannery O'Connor, Truman Capote and Tennessee Williams" (340–42). Richard Ruland and Malcolm Bradbury, in their historical overview of American literature, argue that American novelists were influenced by Gustave Flaubert and the Russian realists, who "bred new grotesquerie, and the new 'realism'" (142). They cite the prominence of these elements in the writings of Mark Twain, Henry James, and William Faulkner, whose "Gothic perspective" influenced "the work of successors like Eudora Welty, Carson McCullers and Flannery O'Connor" (190, 315).[1] McCullers herself nominates the Russian realists (Dostoevsky, Tolstoy, Gogol, Chekhov, Aksakov, and Turgenev) and Flaubert as the literary antecedents of the southern grotesque and implicitly acknowledges their influence on her own work; she also regards Faulkner's *Sound and the Fury* and *As I Lay Dying* as the major contemporary examples of this southern grotesque genre ("Flowering Dream," "Russian Realists"). For Irving Malin, the tradition, which he calls gothic, stems from, among others, Nathaniel Hawthorne's *Blithedale Romance* and Melville's *Moby Dick*, and is later found in the new gothic writers, among whom he includes McCullers, Capote, and O'Connor.

Although there is critical consensus as to the sources and the practitioners of the grotesque, the discrepant terminology used in the various accounts to describe the type of writing McCullers practices and that is typical of much southern writing is already apparent: "realist," "gothic," "grotesque." O'Connor, who, with McCullers, is said to belong to the second generation of renaissance writers, wryly notes the inconsistencies of terminology: "[A]nything that comes out of the South is going to be called grotesque by the Northern reader, unless it is grotesque, in which case it is going to be called realistic" (*Mystery and Manners* 40). McCullers, in her discussion of terminology in "The Russian Realists and Southern Literature," observes that "[i]n the South during the past fifteen years a genre of writing has come about that is sufficiently homogeneous to have led critics to label it 'the Gothic School.'" However, after pondering the term "gothic," she chooses to reject it: "This tag . . . is unfortunate. The effect of a Gothic tale may be similar to that of a Faulkner in its evocation of horror, beauty, and emotional ambivalence—but this effect evolves from opposite sources; in the former the means used are romantic or supernatural, in the latter a peculiar and intense realism. Modern Southern writing seems rather to be indebted to Russian literature, to be the progeny of the Russian realists" (258). McCullers is perhaps unique in her preference for the term "realist" to describe southern writing.

Those McCullers commentators (Malin, Robert Phillips, Margaret McDowell, and Frances Kestler) who label southern writing "gothic" add the English gothic novel of the eighteenth century to the list of precedents. Phillips, in his examination of the "gothic architecture" in *The Member of the Wedding*, distinguishes between the two gothic genres: although both are violent in theme, the southern gothic makes no use of supernatural elements or of tombs and dungeons, unlike its English ancestor ("Gothic Architecture" 59–60). Malin, Phillips, and Kestler also point to the influence of Freudian psychoanalytic theory on the southern gothic. Kestler contends that Freud played a crucial role "in changing the methods by which authors handled character, since he was concerned with uncovering the underlying reasons for emotions, reactions, and behavior" (30).[2] As a result, Malin observes, in the new gothic novel "order breaks down: . . . identity is blurred, sex is twisted" (9).

While these commentators have located McCullers's fiction in the American gothic school of Edgar Allan Poe and Faulkner and/or the tradition of the English gothic, more recently McCullers has been considered in a separate tradition, that is, as a part of a specifically *female* gothic tradition. In her 1977 study *Literary Women*, Ellen Moers, defining gothic writing as a style in which "fantasy dominates over reality, the strange over the commonplace, and the supernatural over the natural," rejects the proposition that McCullers belongs "to the Southern American Gothic school of which William Faulkner is the notorious advertisement." Instead, Moers places McCullers in "a tradition at least as feminine as regional," which traces a genealogy comprising Ann Radcliffe, Mary Shelley, Emily Brontë, and Christina Rosetti, as well as Isak Dinesen (90, 109).[3] Juliann Fleenor, in her introduction to *The Female Gothic*, puts McCullers in similar company, that is, with Radcliffe and the Brontës, and adds O'Connor and Doris Lessing (Fleenor 11).

Other critics, such as Louise Gossett, Van O'Connor, Joseph Millichap, and Pratibha Nagpal, prefer the term "grotesque" to describe McCullers's and, more broadly, southern writing. Nagpal and Van O'Connor, for example, agree that the grotesque is a response to a world of violence and upheaval. Millichap attempts to theorize the relationship of the grotesque to modernist angst in "Distorted Matter and Disjunctive Forms: The Grotesque as Modernist Genre," and he considers the work of James Joyce, Eliot, and Franz Kafka, as well as Faulkner, McCullers, and O'Connor. Millichap's thesis is, in sum, that "in the twisted features of the Grotesque the Modernist writer discerned disjunctive forms capable of ordering the fragmentation and alienation of the modern world" (339).

Alan Spiegel, who, before Millichap, sought to theorize the grotesque in southern fiction, is perhaps the only commentator to distinguish it from the older (English) tradition of the gothic novel: "The gothic gesture takes place outside of society in a nightmare setting, while the grotesque gesture takes place within society in the daylight setting of ordinary communal activity" (433).[4] Spiegel stresses the former's supernatural features, none of which are present in McCullers's texts.[5]

Nonetheless, what almost all accounts of realism or gothic or the grotesque have in common is the idea of *tension* between heterogeneous elements.[6] McCullers describes the writings of the Russian realists and southern writing in terms of juxtaposition: "The technique briefly is this: a bold and outwardly callous juxtaposition of the tragic with the humorous, the immense with the trivial, the sacred with the bawdy, the whole soul of a man with a materialistic detail" ("Russian Realists" 258). McDowell's description of McCullers's gothic novels also defines the gothic mode as the "combination of the violent and comic, and [the] abrogation of the world of the rational" (51). For Richard Cook also, it is by "exaggerating rather than resolving contradictions in human experience, [that] the writer, according to McCullers, could reveal the hidden abnormalities in 'normal' life" (102–3).[7] For Ihab Hassan, grotesque contradiction describes the *style* of McCullers's work: "opposition informs the eccentric design of her form" (*Radical Innocence* 205). More general theories of the grotesque also emphasize the unsettling presence of contradiction: in the grotesque mode, "paradox can penetrate to new and unexpected realms of experience, discovering relationships syntax generally obscures" (Harpham 20). It is of course this idea of tension that underpins my own reading of McCullers's fiction.

Notes

INTRODUCTION

1. This is McCullers's observation in "The Russian Realists and Southern Literature" (*Mortgaged Heart* 258) and "The Flowering Dream: Notes on Writing" (*Mortgaged Heart* 287). For examples of similar approaches to the grotesque, see Phillips, "Gothic Architecture"; Rechnitz; Millichap, "Distorted Matter"; Nagpal; Kestler.

2. Further references to these works will appear as *H*, *R*, *M*, and *B*, respectively. I do not consider McCullers's final novel, *Clock Without Hands;* although it deals with homosexuality to some extent, its concerns lie primarily with issues of race and historical memory. However, the model of reading used throughout this study to explore gendered identity is equally useful for future readings not only of race but also of class, both serious concerns in McCullers's work. Also, because I am chiefly concerned with McCullers's novels, her poetry, short stories, and plays will only be referred to in passing.

3. In her bibliographic study James lists those commentaries on McCullers published in the 1990s: Carr's monograph *Understanding Carson McCullers* and several articles: Chamlee; McBride; Champion; Kissel; Taetzsch; J. Whitt; Stafford; Vande Kieft; and Budick, as well as Clark and Friedman, which appeared while James's monograph was in press. However, the majority of the essays in Clark and Friedman's book have appeared previously, although the following three essays were written specifically for their collection: Paulson; T. Davis; and Kenschaft.

4. Carr's notion of alienation recalls Anderson's "Book of the Grotesque" in *Winesburg, Ohio.*

5. See Baldanza (for a rather quirky account of Platonic love in McCullers's

shorter fiction); Hassan, "Carson McCullers" (reappearing in slightly altered form in Hassan, *Radical Innocence* 205–9); Eisinger; Phillips, "Gothic Architecture"; Paden; Bauerly; Frazier; Thomas; M. Whitt; Johstoneaux; McBride; Vande Kieft.

6. James also makes this point (7).

7. For example, Carlton; Sosnoski.

8. See, for example, Kahane on *The Ballad of the Sad Café*'s Miss Amelia, in "Maternal Legacy" 244, and in "Gothic Mirror" 347–48. Segrest writes, with regard to McCullers's writing, that "when characters . . . swallow that self-hatred uncritically they become what literary critics call *grotesque*" (107).

9. See White 90; Carlton.

10. See also Hassan, "Idea of Adolescence," *Radical Innocence,* and "Post-War Fiction"; Fiedler, *End to Innocence* 191–210; Carpenter 316; Johnson 6.

11. Howard, for example, finds "slightly perverse . . . the loving portrait Carson McCullers paints of female adolescence, a sense that grown-up womanhood is tainted and corrupt and that the pain of being powerless and innocent is preferable to maturity" (20).

12. See also Huf; Dalsimer; Perry; Petry. White likewise explores female adolescence as a category distinct from its male counterpart and, with Ginsberg and Westling, laments Mick's and Frankie's capitulation to conventional womanhood at the expense of their dreams. White argues that while the novel of male initiation may represent "universal" experiences, female adolescence is generally understood in terms of "isolation or freakdom," as Howard's account well illustrates.

13. Spiegel equates adolescence with the grotesque: "the deformed as the *un*formed" (428). Although this chapter is primarily concerned with the female as grotesque, McCullers's male adolescents can be read in a similar fashion in *The Heart Is a Lonely Hunter, Clock Without Hands,* and "Untitled Piece" in *Mortgaged Heart.* Further references will appear as C and "Untitled," respectively.

14. See Phillips, "Gothic Architecture," for a homosexual account of Frankie in *The Member of the Wedding.* A lesbian reading of Miss Amelia Evans in *The Ballad of the Sad Café* is also sustainable; see Kenschaft, who reads McCullers "as a lesbian."

15. For example, Bauerly 74, and the chapter "*Reflections in a Golden Eye*" in Carr's *Understanding Carson McCullers.* Exceptions are Kenschaft's and Paulson's respective essays on male and female homosexuality in McCullers.

16. Fiedler includes Truman Capote, McCullers, J. D. Salinger, and James Baldwin (*Giovanni's Room*). See also Fiedler, *Love and Death* 476.

17. See Sarotte. For further discussion of homosexuality and the military in American literature, including *Reflections in a Golden Eye*, D. H. Lawrence's "The Prussian Officer," and Herman Melville's *Billy Budd*, see Austen, "But for Fate."

The following are further studies of homosexuality and literature that also mention McCullers: Austen briefly examines the irrational, nonreciprocated nature of love in McCullers's texts in *Playing the Game*; Creech, in his study of Melville's *Pierre*, takes a passage from *Reflections in a Golden Eye* as emblematic of the codedness that so often surrounds homosexual desire in the literary text; and Adams claims that McCullers avoids stereotyping homosexual desire by portraying its "freakishness" as a result of the social demand for its repression. See also Spivak in regard to the homosexual as the insane ("Three Feminist Readings" 20). See Richards's account of both gay and lesbian desire in relation to gender and race in all of McCullers's novels (201–49).

18. This concept is employed by De Lauretis. She takes it from Michel Foucault's "technology of gender," which posits that "sexuality is the set of effects produced in bodies, behaviors, and social relations by a certain deployment deriving from a complex political technology" (*History of Sexuality* 127). De Lauretis adds the dimension of sexual difference to Foucault's sexually "neutral" account.

19. See White's summary of these critics (101). On the same topic, Box lists Edmonds (*Carson McCullers*), Evans (*Carson McCullers*), and Madden as critics who "fail to see [Biff] as a positive figure" (121).

CHAPTER 1

1. For a further discussion of the cultural association of women with freaks, see Peterson.

2. Janice, Frankie's brother's fiancée, who is "small and pretty," is another model of ideal womanhood (M 38). In *The Heart Is a Lonely Hunter*, Mick's "models" are Etta Kelly and Baby Wilson. However, they are more properly caricatures of southern femininity discussed in chapter 3.

3. This is emphasized in the dramatization of *The Member of the Wedding* when Mr. Addams refers to the outfit as a "show costume" (act 2, p. 67).

4. The male body is also marked by sexual experience (as well as race) in *Clock Without Hands*. For example, Jester Clane "felt that the old man [his grandfather] knew that he was a virgin" (41). Sherman Pew, at the age of eleven, was raped by his foster father, Mr. Stevens, "so at that period I began to stammer"

(73). Race also marks the body in the short story "The Orphanage" (*Mortgaged Heart*). Hattie explains to the youthful narrator: "If a girl . . . kissed a boy she turned into a coloured person" (64).

5. See also Freud, who writes that "to decapitate = to castrate" ("Medusa's Head" 273).

6. For example, "tightness" is used three times in M 32–33.

7. Berenice adds that she is "caught worse" than either Frankie or John Henry "[b]ecause I am black. . . . Everybody is caught one way or another. But they done drawn completely extra bounds around all coloured people. . . . Sometimes it just about more than we can stand" (M 141).

8. Like the Ancient Mariner, who imagines "the Sun was flecked with bars, / . . . As if through a dungeon-grated he peered / With broad and burning face" (Coleridge 177–80).

9. See also *H* 50.

10. Frankie also feels associated with the town prisoners (M 146).

11. This act of confronting the freak-other, revealing "a monstrous image of self as grotesque body" (Kahane, "Maternal Legacy" 245), also occurs in Flannery O'Connor's *Wise Blood*, as Kahane notes. There, the young man, Hazel Motes, has just such an epiphany as he views the shrunken man in the museum case.

12. For accounts of the history of sideshow freaks, see Fiedler, *Freaks*; Bogdan.

13. Similarly, Henky, in "Correspondence," writes to her penpal: "I am tall and my figure is not good on account of I have grown too rapidly" (*Mortgaged Heart* 163). In "Untitled," Sara's legs are "overgrown and clumsy" and she grows so fast that "she couldn't wear a dress two months before her wrists would be showing and the skirt would be shorter than her bony knees" (112, 117). Yaeger examines the trope of gigantism in southern women's—particularly Eudora Welty's—writing ("Beyond the Hummingbird").

14. They might also be associated with midgets, in their status as "little men," lacking and castrated. See Russo 22–23. This is also implied by Braidotti, who claims that women are culturally perceived not only as "monstrous by excess . . . [but also] monstrous by lack" (*Nomadic Subjects* 83).

15. The examples Westling gives are: Lily Mae Jenkins, John Henry's "transvestism," and his and Frankie's dreams of a world where people can change back and forth, from boys to girls. Flannery O'Connor also uses the figure of the freak show hermaphrodite to suggest the awakening sexual anxiety of a young girl in "A Temple of the Holy Ghost" (97–98).

16. Segrest's description of "normalcy" recalls Bakhtin's description of the classic body (*Rabelais*).

17. See also *H* 48.

18. See also M 14, 33, 133, 149. Furthermore, most of McCullers's adolescents are somehow involved with flight, that liminal state between heaven and earth. I will explore this trope in the next section.

19. This passage anticipates Deleuze and Guattari's assertion that it is "through doors and across thresholds" that the process of "becoming," or change, may be "unleashed" (272). Douglas identifies the power of thresholds residing in their malleability and permeability, which enables transformation (114).

20. Similarly, Jester Clane, in *Clock Without Hands*, must shed his "effeminate" same-sex desire to become a man.

21. See also M 55, 103.

22. Fiedler sees in Frankie's "we of me" fantasy evidence of "the homosexual's sense of exclusion from the family and his [*sic*] uneasiness before heterosexual passion," which he believes is projected in all of McCullers's tomboys (*Love and Death* 333). Westling and White also focus on this "uneasiness," but to suggest that Frankie, by way of the wedding fantasy, hopes to escape adult sexuality (Westling 129; White 104–5). Buchen, on the other hand, claims that Frankie's desire to join the wedding is an incestuous one: "[W]hat she is really asking for is to be a voyeuristic observer of parental sex or an active participant in the bed of her brother—surrogate for that of her father" (24). And Kenschaft believes that Frankie has fallen in love with the "affianced couple."

23. Vande Kieft offers a similar reading (253). Roberts and Snider interpret Frankie's wish to "belong" in Jungian terms. For Snider, the wedding functions as "an archetype of wholeness, symbolizing the union of opposites" (35). This is suggestive of the androgynous unification of masculine and feminine upon which Roberts elaborates (90).

24. Bakhtin writes that the grotesque body "is blended with the world, with animals, with objects. It is cosmic, it represents the entire material bodily world in all its elements" (*Rabelais* 27).

25. Similarly, the grotesque body gains *its* energy from "inside," from the material lower bodily stratum. See, for example, Bakhtin, *Rabelais* 309.

26. The image of (female) flight is also utilized, for example, by Erica Jong in *Fear of Flying* and Angela Carter in *Nights at the Circus* as a similar trope of female freedom. For Jong, this has to do with reclaiming female sexuality for one's self. Carter writes of "the New Age in which no women will be bound down to the ground" (25). Deleuze and Guattari's phrase, "lines of flight," expresses not escape but metamorphosis. See Bogue 110–13.

27. Russo also notes that Earhart "came to stand for all these liberatory aspirations for individual women in the United States in the 1920s and 1930s" (25).

28. Andrew also feels that he must climb down from his almost ecstatic rooftop experience, which leaves him "feeling empty and shamed and more lonesome than anybody else in the world" ("Untitled" 122–23).

29. Concerning Frankie, see, for example, Dalsimer; Gossett. Concerning Mick, see McDowell; Sosnoski.

30. Concerning Frankie, see Westling; Carlton. Concerning Mick, see Spivak, "Three Feminist Readings"; Box.

31. This is the interpretation given by Eisinger 250; Gossett 164; Schorer 282; Dalsimer 26; Snider 42; and Carr, *Understanding Carson McCullers* 75.

CHAPTER 2

1. See Foucault, *History of Sexuality* 101; Weeks, *Sex, Politics and Society* 102; Halperin, *One Hundred Years* 15. All claim that the term came into being at the end of the nineteenth century.

2. Foucault argues that epistemic constructions have naturalized the presumption that to know one's sexuality is to know one's very essence (*History of Sexuality* 69).

3. Foucault, *Use of Pleasure* 220. For accounts of the cultural "silence" about homosexual desire, see Beaver; Sinfield 5f.; Foucault, *History of Sexuality* 27; Sedgwick, *Epistemology* 91–130; Roth.

4. Creech posits a similar reading of this passage (93–94).

5. See, for example, Evans, *Carson McCullers* 63; Carr, *Understanding Carson McCullers* 37.

6. In D. H. Lawrence's "The Prussian Officer," it is spilled red wine that sets in motion a similar chain of events. Lawrence's story is also often compared with *Reflections*. See McDowell 54; Evans's chapter on *Reflections in a Golden Eye* in *Carson McCullers;* Sarotte 83–85.

7. Carr adds that McCullers was familiar with the work of Freud, who believed that all human beings are capable of making a homosexual object-choice.

8. Many readers of *The Heart Is a Lonely Hunter* prefer to understand their relationship as one invested with a failed Christian ethos of brotherly love. Since this chapter will draw on the irony of such love, I would argue that their relationship is not merely brotherly or Platonic. When Antonapoulos is sent to the asylum, "Singer knew that everything was finished" (12), and he is consequently left with "a great aching loneliness" (4). See also Singer's letter to the illiterate Antonapoulos (191), which goes beyond the discourse of mere friendship, of "brotherly love." After Antonapoulos's death, Singer suicides in despair; without

Antonapoulos, Singer is like the "homeless Doppelganger" of McCullers's poem "The Mortgaged Heart" (*Mortgaged Heart* 292).

9. For further discussion, see, for example, Walsh 47; Rechnitz 461; Millichap, "Carson McCullers" 332; Gervin 41; Vande Kieft 253; Baldanza 162; R. Cook 95; Carr, *Understanding Carson McCullers* 64.

10. Further references will appear as "Jockey." No other readers have considered the jockey homosexual, as James also notes (176).

11. McCullers "refuses to draw moral distinctions between different types of love" (Adams 61). Adams goes on to note that "[h]omosexual repression is matched [in *Reflections*] by heterosexual abandon. There is little that is morally honorable in the 'normal' world" (61). See also Austen's discussion (*But for Fate* 358–59).

12. There is of course the odd exception: Berenice's mothering of Frankie in *The Member of the Wedding* and the warmth of the café Miss Amelia creates in *The Ballad of the Sad Café*.

13. Miss Amelia Evans.

14. Mick Kelly, Frankie Addams, Sara of "Untitled Piece," and Henky of "Correspondence."

15. Mick Kelly's mother in *The Heart Is a Lonely Hunter*. See also "The Haunted Boy" (*Mortgaged Heart* 173–85).

16. The young girl is possibly dying in "Breath from the Sky" (*Mortgaged Heart* 54–63). In *The Ballad of the Sad Café*, *Clock Without Hands*, and *The Member of the Wedding*, the mothers of Miss Amelia, Jester Clane, and Frankie Addams are dead.

17. Carlton notes that only Amelia's aunt and a female cousin are mentioned, and "the other females . . . are shadowy figures, without names or faces, unless linked with a male" (60).

18. Once he touches Leonora Penderton, "he was afraid of this sickness no more" (*R* 122).

19. This is Bakhtin commenting on Rabelais's presentation of women. Bakhtin here also emphasizes the corresponding productivity and fertility of female genitals and the womb. See also *Rabelais* 92, 148.

20. René Girard uncovers this bond between men in male rivalry over women in *Deceit, Desire and the Novel*, discussed in Sedgwick, *Between Men* 21. Garber surveys Girard (the heterosexual triangle), Sedgwick (the gay male triangle), and Terry Castle (the lesbian triangle). Garber concludes that what is constitutive of all three analyses is "triangularity" or "bisexuality": "in all three cases it is bisexual triangularity that provokes, explains, and encompasses both

heterosexuality and homosexuality" (*Vice Versa* 428). Given that heterosexuality and homosexuality can be seen as species of a more general bisexuality, Sedgwick's account of the homosexual triangle is more pertinent to this chapter, the focus of which is male-male desire.

21. The exceptions are the convent from which McCullers as a child is excluded, "How I Began to Write" (*Mortgaged Heart* 255–57), the clubs from which Frankie Addams and Mick Kelly are respectively excluded, and the Guides that Sara in "Untitled Piece" leaves after just four days.

22. In her discussion of misogyny in *The Ballad of the Sad Café*, Paulson also comments on the chain gang in terms of Sedgwick's "homosocial."

23. Sedgwick performs a similar reading of leg irons in Charles Dickens's *Great Expectations* (*Between Men* 192–93).

24. This is discussed in chapters 3 and 4.

25. See Foucault, *Use of Pleasure;* Halperin, *One Hundred Years.*

26. Richards writes that it "is perhaps not insignificant that Antonapoulos is Greek, a national and/or ethnic identity frequently linked to male homosexuality because of the region's accepted pederastic relationships during antiquity." He also notes that "Greek" in gay subculture means anal sex (207–8).

27. Weeks writes that "sublimated homosexual feeling was an important factor in binding groups together, from the sanctity of priestly orders to the masculine ethos of military organization" (*Sexuality and Its Discontents* 152). Ernest Jones suggests men enlist in the armed forces in response to "the homosexual desire to be in close relation with masses of men" ("War and Individual Psychology," *Sociological Review* [1915]: 177, quoted in Showalter, *Female Malady* 171). D'Emilio and Freedman write that World War II allowed for "new erotic opportunities that promoted the articulation of a gay identity and the rapid growth of a gay subculture. . . . For a generation of young Americans, the war created a setting in which to experience same-sex love, affection, and sexuality" (289–90).

28. The military is portrayed in a similarly erotic way in Melville's *Billy Budd* and Lawrence's "The Prussian Officer." With regard to "The Prussian Officer," see McDowell 54; Evans, *Carson McCullers* 63; Sarotte 83. With regard to *Billy Budd*, see Evans, *Carson McCullers* 54; Carr, *Understanding Carson McCullers* 37.

29. Similarly, Singer envies one of Antonapoulos's fellow inmates of the asylum "because he lived with Antonapoulos day after day. Singer would have changed places with him joyfully" (*H* 196).

30. Halperin writes that in ancient Greece, the pederast became virile, while

the heterosexual man was "infected by femininity" ("Historicizing the Sexual Body" 250).

31. For a discussion of homosexuality and the military in *Billy Budd*, "The Prussian Officer," and *Reflections in a Golden Eye*, as well as Dennis Murphy's *The Sergeant* and James Purdy's *Eustace Chisholm and the Works*, see Austen, "But for Fate."

32. See for example, Carr, *Understanding Carson McCullers* 40; R. Cook 57, 48–49.

33. Biff Brannon provides a more complex representation of virility because of the simple fact that he often appears as feminine. He nevertheless displays similar all-male traits. He has, for instance, a "black and heavy beard" (*H* 17; see also 33, 89). Biff needs to shave frequently and has "dark, hairy armpits" (*H* 198). Another example of virility is Major Langdon, who even has "hairy fists" (*R* 41).

34. As Penderton is by the thought of Williams (*R* 93).

35. Sarotte argues that "*the homoerotic delinquent boy becomes the caricature of the American virile ideal*," and he cites Marvin Macy as his example (189; emphasis in original).

36. Sedgwick locates similar portrayals in *Billy Budd* where men, "rather than having erections, tend to turn into them, or to turn each other into them" (*Epistemology* 125).

37. This reflects Freud's claim that the male spectator is "stiff with terror" at the sight of Medusa, who threatens castration ("Medusa's Head" 273).

38. Jester Clane is also impotent (C 41). With relevance to the Captain, Gilbert and Gubar find a link between the military/warfare and impotence in post–World War I literature: T. S. Eliot's Fisher King, Hemingway's Jake Barnes, Ford Madox Ford's O Nine Morgan, and Lawrence's Clifford Chatterly (260).

39. Showalter notes that Charcot believed "hysterical men were . . . impotent" (*Female Malady* 172).

40. Roth, in a discussion of the displacement of homosexuality in the literary text, cites Jean-Paul Aron's assertion that many writers worked by "erasing homosexuality and substituting impotence" (272–73).

41. Nightmares are another symptom of male hysteria. See Showalter, *Female Malady* 174. See also Captain Penderton's nightmare of the great dark bird in *Reflections in a Golden Eye* (54), which is echoed in Anacleto's vision of the golden-eyed peacock from which the title of the novel is drawn (86–87).

42. This cross is first mentioned in *H* 10.

43. Evans rejects this reading of the "thing" as a cross for "it is Singer rather

than Antonapoulos who has been endowed with Christlike qualities" ("Case of the Silent Singer" 193). However, this does not rule out another person making a religious offering. Indeed, it supports the idea that Singer would dream of another's doing so.

44. See, for example, Champion; Dodd; Durham.

45. See also Evans, "Case of the Silent Singer" 193.

46. Similarly, Bitsy Barlow's hands are "small, strong and calloused" ("Jockey" 107).

47. Carr writes that McCullers had a passing acquaintance with Anderson (*Lonely Hunter* 145). Evans compares *The Heart Is a Lonely Hunter* to "Queer," and a scene in *The Ballad of the Sad Café* to "The Egg," *Winesburg, Ohio* (*Carson McCullers* 54, 135). No one comments on Anderson's story "Hands" in *Winesburg, Ohio* with regard to McCullers's works.

48. This recalls Biff's and Penderton's respective yearnings for the homosocial societies of ancient Greece and the Middle Ages, and also the Platonic eroticization of the pedagogic relationship Sarotte discusses (65).

49. See also Evans, "Case of the Silent Singer" 193.

50. According to Creed, mutism is another symptom of the paralysis of "phallic panic" (130).

51. As does Private Williams with regard to Leonora Penderton. This will not be discussed since this chapter focuses on male-male desire. However, it provides further evidence of how McCullers avoids sexual stereotypes.

52. Freud claims that "inverts," "proceeding from a basis of narcissism, . . . look for a young man who resembles themselves" ("Sexual Aberrations" 56n. 1).

53. See also Halperin: with the work of Freud and Havelock Ellis, "deciphering what a person's sexual orientation 'really' was [became] independent of beguiling appearances" (*One Hundred Years* 16).

54. As Sedgwick so cannily writes: "I do not believe that identification and desire are necessarily more closely linked in same-sex than in cross-sex relationships. . . . I certainly do not believe that any given man must be assumed to have more in common with any other given man than he can possibly have in common with any given woman" (*Epistemology* 159).

55. Singer is also reflected in a window (*H* 282).

56. M. Whitt also makes this point (26). Biff reacts similarly to the death of his wife, Alice: he starts to wear her perfume and her lemon hair rinse (*H* 199–200).

57. Freud also makes a connection between masochism and impotence and masturbation ("Economic Problem of Masochism" 416).

58. Penderton also chooses to wear "the coarsest sleeping garments" (*R* 123–

24). Evans adds that Penderton "derives satisfaction from Major Langdon's company," although he knows Langdon is having an affair with his wife (*Carson McCullers* 65).

59. Another out-of-body experience occurs later, when Penderton "was in a state of sharpened sensitivity close to delirium" (*R* 117).

60. Penderton also hopes that Williams will be court-martialed, and he envisions them both "wrestling together naked, body to body, in a fight to death" (*R* 14, 77). Private Williams is also sadistic: he commits murder over some manure, for which he shows no remorse. He also picks a fight in the barracks for no reason (*R* 91, 120).

61. He is also described as "nervous," "uneasy," "fidgety," "restless," and "irritated" (*R* 52, 33, 28, 14, 13).

62. And "craving" (*R* 110).

63. These tropes are also found in *Billy Budd*, "The Prussian Officer," and "Hands" (in *Winesburg, Ohio*). Billy, the Orderly, and the children in "Hands" are the supposed innocents of nature, corrupted by the worldly homosexual. These tropes partake in those of secrecy/disclosure and knowledge/ignorance, noted at the beginning of this chapter.

64. Eisinger believes that Williams belongs in the "nature" category, which "illustrate[s] the healthy principle of natural animality." Penderton is in the "culture" category, whose members are "full of self-doubts and adept at self-torture" (252). Similarly, Evans describes Williams as "the man of nature" who is associated with sexual health (*Carson McCullers* 65, 71). Rechnitz describes Williams in a similar way: an "a-moral, near-animal," he is "[t]he only one at all capable of loving." By contrast, Penderton is a "moral cripple" (455). See also Carr's chapter "Reflections in a Golden Eye" (in *Understanding Carson McCullers*), for example, pp. 41, 49; McDowell 54.

65. Furthermore, Penderton is twice described as a doll, suggesting lifelessness and the mechanical (*R* 72, 113).

66. This is suggested by his fear of Firebird and his horror of having the forest exposed in his garden (*R* 67, 12–13).

67. See, for example, his sadistic treatment of Firebird and his cruel treatment of a kitten, which he stuffs in a mailbox (*R* 16).

68. See also the references to "the dark sphere of his consciousness" (*R* 11, 23).

69. And Evans claims that Private Williams "is not *healthy*: a tendency to voyeurism is scarcely an attribute of the Noble Savage" (*Carson McCullers* 67). Roberts also expresses doubt about Williams's "innocence" (88).

70. In a 1935 letter, Freud writes: "[W]e consider [homosexuality] to be a

variation of the sexual function produced by a certain arrest of sexual development" (quoted in Abelove 59).

71. See also Bitsy Barlow ("Jockey" 103).

72. Furthermore, "effeminacy might be attached to almost any deviant perspective," such as Jews, Catholics, and anarchists (Sinfield 78). In *The Ballad of the Sad Café*, for example, Morris Finestein is Jewish and described as prissy and one "who cried if you called him Christ-killer" (14). It is rumored in *The Heart Is a Lonely Hunter* that Singer too is Jewish (77, 121, 177, 263). And, immediately after McCullers describes Biff's new Orientalist (associated with dandyism) interior design, and his use of Alice's perfume and lemon hair rinse, the reader learns that Biff is "an eighth part Jew" (*H* 199).

73. Richards discusses this in his chapter on McCullers.

74. And see Roth 275–76. This will be discussed in detail in the following chapter. Biff's increasing femininity is the subject of chapter 4.

75. There is also an earlier reference to Penderton's "attempt to square the circle" (*R* 15).

76. Bordo discusses the "deep associations of masculinity as active, . . . and femininity as passive . . . [which] underlie the equation of the penetrability of femininity" (288). However, as both Bordo and Gatens incisively point out, there is no reason to consider the vagina a passive receptacle—it can be perceived as actively embracing the penis. See Bordo 288–89; Gatens 152.

77. This image also recalls Lawrence's Prussian Officer, who is similarly "violated" by his strange desire: "[T]he young soldier's being had penetrated through the officer's stiffened discipline, and perturbed the man in him" (10).

CHAPTER 3

1. Castle attests not only to a tradition of carnival masquerade in American southern life but also to "the persistence of the carnival/masquerade theme in Southern writing from Poe to James Purdy," of which McCullers may have been aware (339). Castle also mentions Isak Dinesen's "Carnival" as an example of a more recent work with a masquerade as its setting. In a review ("Isak Dinesen: Winter's Tales"), McCullers notes Dinesen's use of "[m]asquerade [and] trickery" (*Mortgaged Heart* 272). The long tradition of carnivalesque masquerade is founded in the European folk culture of antiquity and the Middle Ages (Bakhtin, *Rabelais* 39).

2. To cross-dress is literally to transgress. The Bible declares: "The woman shall not wear that which pertaineth unto a man, neither shall a man put on a

woman's garment: for all that do so are abomination unto the Lord thy God" (Deut. 22:5).

3. Gilbert and Gubar call McCullers "an inveterate cross-dresser" (354).

4. Westling is responding to George Fitzhugh's 1854 statement that the southern lady's "weakness is her strength, and her true art is to cultivate and improve that weakness" (17).

5. See Westling 120–26; Millichap, "Carson McCullers"; Griffith; Walsh. Gervin explores the resemblance between Amelia and the Greek goddess Artemis, another virgin huntress. According to Warner, Artemis "stood above all for fierce autonomy, for which her unassailable virginity was the sign" (202).

6. See, for example, Heinrich von Kleist's 1808 play, *Penthesilea*.

7. See Irigaray, *This Sex* 170–91.

8. For Evans, for example, it is "her failure to accept the vital principle" (*Carson McCullers* 135). See also Robert Phillips, "Painful Love: Carson McCullers' Parable," *Southwest Review* 51 (1966): 80–86, quoted in James 83. McDowell writes that she is "afraid to assume her full sexual identity" (73).

9. Biff well expresses Garber's claim that male-to-female drag declares "that the outside (the performer's clothing) is feminine and his inside (the body inside the clothing) is masculine, and, at the same time, that the outside (the performer's body) is masculine and his inside (his 'essence' or 'self') is feminine" (*Vested Interests* 152).

10. See also "Mortgaged Heart," which expresses a similar sentiment: "the dead can claim / The lover's senses, the mortgaged heart" (292).

11. There are significant problems with the idea of the appropriation of the feminine, discussed in chapter 4.

12. Biff's "stiffening" recalls Freud's discussion of male fear of castration, which "makes the spectator stiff with terror," as well as of male erection as a defiance of castration ("Medusa's Head" 273).

13. See also Holmlund 217; Heath 55–56.

14. As Holmlund suggests, "muscles are costume enough" (222).

15. See also *H* 17, 33, 153, 189.

16. See also Butler, *Gender Trouble* 134–41; Butler, "Performative Acts" 270–82. As regards this norm, for Freud, the development of both the little boy and the little girl is regulated by the incest taboo and the Oedipus complex ("Ego and Id"). See Butler's *Gender Trouble:* sexual identity is also regulated through "compulsory heterosexuality" (59–77).

17. Gatens writes that in Freud's view, "femininity" is characterized by "passivity, masochism, narcissism, envy, shame" (152).

18. Even the double "Miss" of her nickname reinforces her idealized maidenhood.

19. Irigaray adds that "a man is a man from the outset" (*This Sex* 134). However, I have argued that in McCullers's text, men too perform masculinity and so must "become" men.

20. Michele Montrelay, "Inquiry into Femininity," *m/f* 1 (1978): 93, quoted in Doane 82.

21. Westling is writing specifically about Frankie.

22. The notion of the fool as feminist tactician emerged in a conversation with Jane Marcus at Cambridge University, Cambridge, England, in 1994. Traditionally, the fool in carnival or literature was always male. See Bauer 12; N. Davis 140–41.

23. Bauer draws a productive analogy between the fool and several nineteenth-century American literary heroines to argue that "these women provide the means of unmasking dominant codes. Stupidity (a form of resistance) forces the unspoken repressions into the open, thus making them vulnerable to interpretation, contradiction and dialogue" (11).

24. Lisabeth During drew my attention to this issue in a conversation, School of Philosophy, University of New South Wales, Sydney, May 1997. See the chapter "Tennyson's *Princess:* One Bride for Seven Brothers" in Sedgwick's *Between Men* 118–33, for a discussion of Tennyson in this light.

25. For discussions of Amelia's magical powers, see Griffith 49; Westling 124; Millichap, "Carson McCullers" 333.

26. This is Barnes's description of the transvestite Doctor O'Connor in *Nightwood.*

27. This suggests Lacan's claim in "Signification of the Phallus" that woman must "seem" to be the phallus, as well as Irigaray's conceptualization of the conservative form of masquerade in *Speculum*.

CHAPTER 4

1. The other two were two parts male and two parts female.

2. Freud refers to Plato's myth as a "theory" ("Beyond the Pleasure Principle" 331–32).

3. For various readings of Woolf's concept of androgyny, see Showalter, "Virginia Woolf and the Flight into Androgyny" (Showalter, *A Literature of Their Own* 263–97); Moi, "Introduction: Who's Afraid of Virginia Woolf? Feminist Readings of Woolf" (Moi 1–18); Weil 145–59. See also Woolf's essay "Coleridge as Critic" (Woolf, *Essays* 221–25).

4. For an account of this criticism, see Showalter, *A Literature of Their Own*; Secor.

5. Schor's term referring to the erasure of sexual difference so that "a single universal history is presumed to cover both sexes" ("Dreaming Dissymmetry" 107).

6. See also *H* 23–24, 119–20, 207.

7. The exceptions are White, who applies the term "androgynous" to Amelia as well as Biff (100); and Rechnitz, who describes her as "a mixture of man-woman" (459).

8. See Westling 123; Millichap, "Carson McCullers" 334.

9. See Box 122–23; Kestler 31; and Evans, *Carson McCullers* 47–48.

10. Biff's attraction to the adolescent Mick, who is "as much like an overgrown boy than a girl," is echoed in his daydreams of "thin naked little boys, the half-grown children" (*H* 119, 110).

11. Carr even suggests that he is the "true" (androgynous) Christ-figure of the novel (*Understanding Carson McCullers* 32). (Singer is more commonly regarded as the Christ-figure. See Evans, *Carson McCullers* 41; Durham; Schorer 278; M. Whitt 25.) For Christ as an androgynous figure, see Weil 64; Heilbrun, *Toward a Recognition* 17–20; Daly 88.

12. Dodd makes a similar claim: Biff's "sexual needs are answered by his supplying in himself the female as well as the male role" (208). Eisinger writes that after Alice's death, Biff "becomes the unitary expression of both the male and female principles" (249).

13. See also Taetzsch, who maintains that "his developing androgyny is still contaminated by Alice's presence" (193). Interestingly, in Ovid's account of Hermaphroditus, the feminine, in the form of Salmacis, is likewise considered a contaminant, but to manhood, not to a "developing androgyny" (93).

14. Even when Alice was alive, "there was no distinctive point about her on which he could fasten his attention. . . . When he was away from her there was no one feature that stood out in his mind and he remembered her as a complete, unbroken figure" (*H* 17–18).

15. This idea is also reflected in "Mortgaged Heart."

16. Hugh McPherson, "Carson McCullers: Lonely Huntress," *Tamarack Review* 11 (spring 1959): 31, quoted in Box 121; Eisinger 249.

17. On this point, see Carlton 60.

18. See also Bakhtin, *Rabelais* 21, 308. The notion of pregnancy is also apparent in Woolf's conceptualization of androgyny where she writes that "[i]t is when fusion takes place that the mind is fully fertilized" (*Room of One's Own* 92).

19. See also Bakhtin, *Rabelais* 25, 26, 50, 52, 92.

20. Note also that the mothers of Frankie and Miss Amelia died in childbirth.

21. See also Bakhtin, *Rabelais* 242, 243.

22. See also Russo 56, 63.

23. Amelia's case is interesting, for when she performs womanliness with a vengeance, she is at the height of her powers, as explored in the previous chapter. But when she becomes unmanned/castrated, she is left "only" a woman.

24. Dugs are human breasts that are withered and old, doubly emphasizing the unproductive, unnourishing figure of Tiresias. This image might also recall the old hags of *Rabelais*. However, it must be remembered that they are "pregnant."

25. Robert S. Phillips, "Painful Love: Carson McCullers's Parable," *Southwest Review* 51 (1966): 82, quoted in James 82.

26. For example, Alison Langdon and Leonora Penderton in *Reflections in a Golden Eye*, Alice Brannon in *The Heart Is a Lonely Hunter*, and Berenice Sadie Brown in *The Member of the Wedding*.

27. Stallybrass and White employ hybridity for their analysis of English cultural history and define it as the carnivalesque process of "inmixing" whereby "self and other become enmeshed in an inclusive, heterogeneous, dangerously unstable zone" (193).

28. See also Garber, *Vice Versa* 214, 218.

29. Weil also draws on Schlegel's distinction between two types of irony (31–59). Haraway's concept of irony is also useful here: "Irony is about contradictions that do not resolve into larger wholes, even dialectically, about the tension of holding incompatible things together because both or all are necessary and true" (65). See also Weil regarding Haraway and irony (160–61).

30. Like the freak show hermaphrodite in O'Connor's "A Temple of the Holy Ghost," McCullers's hermaphrodite remains clothed. See chapter 1 above for an account of the hermaphrodite as an adolescent fantasy. See Kahane, "Maternal Legacy," for an account of the hermaphrodite in O'Connor. See Westling for a comparison of the use to which O'Connor and McCullers put this figure.

31. Daly likens androgyny to an image of "John Travolta and Farrah Fawcett-Majors scotch-taped together" (xi).

32. An intriguing example is Rich, who takes great pains to assert Biff's masculinity in order to avoid any possibility that he might be a "deviant." She bends over backward to "justify" Biff's feminine operations: he sews because he is a "practical man and not confined by the chauvinistic attitude that it is woman's work"; his opulent decor reveals "aesthetic appreciation and a romantic nature"; he wears Alice's perfume as a reminder of the past. In sum, all Biff's feminine traits "reveal his strength; Jake [Blount] recognizes and respects this, for al-

though he jeers at Biff about his being a capitalist, he never ridicules his perfume" (118–19).

33. Similarly, Flannery O'Connor believes that to "know oneself is, above all, to know what one lacks" (*Mystery and Manners* 35).

CONCLUSION

1. For accounts of McCullers's novels as social commentary, see Millichap, "Realistic Structure"; Fiedler, *Love and Death* 478; Korenman; Hassan, "Carson McCullers" 315; Champion; S. Cook 156–58; Miles 133–34. With regard to class and gender in *The Heart Is a Lonely Hunter*, see Spivak, "Three Feminist Readings." With regard to race and sexuality in *Clock Without Hands*, see Richards 240–49; T. Davis; Yaeger, *Dirt and Desire*. With regard to disability and the grotesque more broadly, see Thomson, *Extraordinary Bodies*.

2. See McHale.

CRITICAL SURVEY

1. See also Hassan, *Contemporary American Literature* 67.

2. Freud visited the United States only once, in 1909. For an account of Freud's relationship with America, see Abelove.

3. See McCullers's articles on Isak Dinesen ("Isak Dinesen: *Winter's Tales*" and "Isak Dinesen: In Praise of Radiance") in *Mortgaged Heart*. For a discussion of Dinesen and McCullers, see Phillips, "Dinesen's 'Monkey'"; McDowell 51; Westling 120–22.

4. Spiegel's distinction between the southern grotesque and the gothic is similar to Phillips's distinction in "Gothic Architecture" between the English and American gothic.

5. At a stretch, it could be argued that in *The Ballad of the Sad Café* Amelia Evans's belief in numerology, for example, could align itself with the supernatural. More accurately, however, this belief belongs to folkloric superstition. Spiegel usefully claims that the grotesque in southern writing "refers to a type of character," not to "a particular quality of a story . . . nor to its mood . . . nor to its mode of expression," and it occurs in "either a physically or mentally deformed figure" (428). Moers claims that in the modern female gothic, "freaks" have replaced monsters (108).

6. Malin, for example, locates the tension as "between ego and super-ego, self and society" (4).

7. Cook is responding to "Russian Realists."

Works Cited

WORKS BY CARSON MCCULLERS

The Ballad of the Sad Café. 1951. London: Penguin, 1963.

Clock Without Hands. 1961. London: Penguin, 1965.

Collected Stories of Carson McCullers: Including "The Member of the Wedding" and "The Ballad of the Sad Café." Boston: Houghton, 1987.

The Heart Is a Lonely Hunter. 1940. London: Penguin, 1961.

Illumination and Night Glare: The Unfinished Autobiography of Carson McCullers. Ed. Carlos Dews. Madison: U of Wisconsin P, 1999.

The Member of the Wedding. 1946. London: Penguin, 1962.

The Member of the Wedding: A Play. New York: New Directions, 1951.

The Mortgaged Heart. 1972. London: Penguin, 1975.

Reflections in a Golden Eye. 1941. London: Penguin, 1967.

OTHER WORKS CITED

Abelove, Henry. "Freud, Male Homosexuality, and the Americans." *Dissent* (Winter 1986): 59–69.

Adams, Stephen. *The Homosexual as Hero in Contemporary Fiction*. London: Vision, 1980.

Anandan, Prathima. "Corporeal Realities: Reading Carson McCullers's *The Member of the Wedding* as an *Entiwicklungsroman*." *Carson McCullers Society Newsletter* 4 (2001): 1–5.

Anderson, Sherwood. *Winesburg, Ohio*. 1919. London: Picador, 1988.

Austen, Roger. "But for Fate and Ban: Homosexual Villains and Victims in the Military." *College English* 36.3 (1974): 352–59.

——. *Playing the Game: The Homosexual Novel in America*. Indianapolis: Bobbs, 1977.

Bakhtin, Mikhail. *The Dialogic Imagination: Four Essays by M. M. Bakhtin*. Trans. Caryl Emerson and Michael Holquist. Austin: U of Texas P, 1981.

——. "Discourse in the Novel." *The Dialogic Imagination: Four Essays by M. M. Bakhtin*. Trans. Caryl Emerson and Michael Holquist. Austin: U of Texas P, 1981. 259–422.

——. *Rabelais and His World*. Trans. Helene Iswolsky. Bloomington: Indiana UP, 1984.

Baldanza, Frank, Jr. "Plato in Dixie." *Georgia Review* 12.2 (1958): 151–67.

Barnes, Djuna. *Nightwood*. 1936. London: Faber, 1985.

Baudelaire, Charles. *The Painter of Modern Life and Other Essays*. Trans. and ed. Jonathan Mayne. London: Phaidon, 1964.

Bauer, Dale. *Feminist Dialogics: A Theory of Failed Community*. Albany: State U of New York P, 1988.

Bauerly, Donna. "Themes of Eros and Agape in the Major Fiction of Carson McCullers." *Pembroke Magazine* 20 (1988): 72–76.

Beaver, Harold. "Homosexual Signs (In Memory of Roland Barthes)." *Critical Inquiry* 8 (1981): 99–119.

Bogdan, Robert. *Freak Show: Presenting Human Oddities for Amusement and Profit*. Chicago: U of Chicago P, 1988.

Bogue, Ronald. *Deleuze and Guattari*. London: Routledge, 1989.

Bordo, Susan. "Reading the Male Body." *The Male Body: Features, Destinies, Exposures*. Ed. Laurence Goldstein. Ann Arbor: U of Michigan P, 1994. 265–306.

Box, Patricia S. "Androgyny and the Musical Vision: A Study of Two Novels of Carson McCullers." *Southern Quarterly* 17.1 (1978): 117–23.

Braidotti, Rosi. *Nomadic Subjects: Embodiment and Sexual Difference in Contemporary Feminist Theory*. New York: Columbia UP, 1994.

——. *Patterns of Dissonance: A Study of Women in Contemporary Philosophy*. Cambridge: Polity, 1991.

Broughton, Panthea Reid. "Rejection of the Feminine in Carson McCullers' *The Ballad of the Sad Café*." *Twentieth Century Literature* 20.1 (1974): 34–43.

Buchen, Irving H. "Carson McCullers, A Case of Convergence." *Bucknell Review* 21 (1973): 15–28.

Budick, Emily Miller. "The Mother Tongue: Carson McCullers." *Engendering Romance: Women Writers and the Hawthorne Tradition, 1850–1990*. New Haven: Yale UP, 1994. 143–61.

Butler, Judith. *Bodies That Matter: On the Discursive Limits of "Sex."* New York: Routledge, 1993.

———. *Gender Trouble: Feminism and the Subversion of Identity*. New York: Routledge, 1990.

———. "Performative Acts and Gender Constitution: An Essay in Phenomenology and Feminist Theory." *Performing Feminisms: Feminist Critical Theory and Theatre*. Ed. Sue-Ellen Case. Baltimore: Johns Hopkins UP, 1990. 270–82.

Carlton, Ann. "Beyond Gothic and Grotesque: A Feminist View of Three Female Characters of Carson McCullers." *Pembroke Magazine* 20 (1988): 54–62.

Carpenter, Frederic I. "The Adolescent in American Fiction." *English Journal* 46.6 (1957): 313–19.

Carr, Virginia Spencer. *The Lonely Hunter: A Biography of Carson McCullers*. New York: Carroll, 1975.

———. *Understanding Carson McCullers*. Columbia: U of South Carolina P, 1990.

Carter, Angela. *Nights at the Circus*. London: Chatto, 1984.

Castle, Terry. *Masquerade and Civilization: The Carnivalesque in Eighteenth-Century English Culture and Fiction*. Stanford: Stanford UP, 1986.

Chamlee, Kenneth D. "Cafés and Community in Three Carson McCullers Novels." *Studies in American Fiction* 18 (1990): 233–40.

Champion, Laurie. "Black and White Christs in Carson McCullers's *The Heart Is a Lonely Hunter*." *Southern Literary Journal* 24 (1991): 47–52.

Chopin, Kate. *The Awakening*. 1899. London: Women's Press, 1978.

Cixous, Hélène. "Castration or Decapitation?" Trans. Annette Kuhn. *Signs* 7.1 (1981): 41–55.

Clark, Beverly, and Melvin J. Friedman, eds. *Critical Essays on Carson McCullers*. New York: Hall, 1996.

Clark, Katerina, and Michael Holquist. *Mikhail Bakhtin*. Cambridge: Harvard UP, 1984.

Coleridge, Samuel T. "The Rime of the Ancient Mariner." 1816. *Coleridge: The Poems*. Ed. John Beer. London: Dent, 1974. 173–89.

Cook, Richard M. *Carson McCullers*. New York: Ungar, 1975.

Cook, Sylvia Jenkins. *From Tobacco Road to Route 66: The Southern Poor White in Fiction*. Chapel Hill: U of North Carolina P, 1976.

Creech, James. *Closet Writing/Gay Reading: The Case of Melville's* Pierre. Chicago: U of Chicago P, 1993.

Creed, Barbara. "Phallic Panic: Male Hysteria and *Dead Ringers*." *Screen* 31.2 (1990): 125–46.

Cullingford, Elizabeth Butler. "The Historical Poetics of Excrement: Yeats's Crazy Jane and the Irish Bishops." *A Dialogue of Voices: Feminist Literary Theory and Bakhtin*. Ed. Karen Hohne and Helen Wussow. Minneapolis: U of Minnesota P, 1994. 20–41.

Dalsimer, Katherine. "Preadolescence: *The Member of the Wedding*." *Female Adolescence: Psychoanalytic Reflections on Works of Literature*. New Haven: Yale UP, 1986. 13–26.

Daly, Mary. *Gyn/Ecology: The Metaethics of Radical Feminism*. London: Women's Press, 1979.

Davis, Natalie Zemon. "Women on Top." *Society and Culture in Early Modern France*. 1965. Cambridge: Polity, 1987. 124–51.

Davis, Thadious M. "Erasing the 'We of Me' and Rewriting the Racial Script: Carson McCullers's Two *Member[s] of the Wedding*." *Critical Essays on Carson McCullers*. Ed. Beverly Lyon Clark and Melvin J. Friedman. New York: Hall, 1996. 206–19.

De Lauretis, Teresa. *Technologies of Gender: Essays on Theory, Film, and Fiction*. Bloomington: Indiana UP, 1987.

Deleuze, Gilles, and Félix Guattari. *A Thousand Plateaus: Capitalism and Schizophrenia*. Trans. Brian Massumi. London: Athlone, 1988.

D'Emilio, John, and Estelle B. Freedman. *Intimate Matters: A History of Sexuality in America*. New York: Harper, 1988.

Derrida, Jacques. " . . . That Dangerous Supplement. . . . " *Of Grammatology*. Trans. Gayatri Chakravorty Spivak. Baltimore: Johns Hopkins UP, 1976. 141–64.

Doane, Mary Ann. "Film and the Masquerade: Theorising the Female Spectator." *Screen* 23.3–4 (1982): 74–87.

Dodd, Wayne. "The Development of Theme through Symbol in the Novels of Carson McCullers." *Georgia Review* 17 (1963): 206–13.

Douglas, Mary. *Purity and Danger: An Analysis of Concepts of Pollution and Taboo*. London: Routledge, 1966.

Durham, Frank. "God and No God in *The Heart Is a Lonely Hunter*." *South Atlantic Quarterly* 56 (1957): 494–99.

Edmonds, Dale. *Carson McCullers*. Austin: Steck, 1969.

———. "'Correspondence': A 'Forgotten' Carson McCullers Short Story." *Studies in Short Fiction* 9 (1972): 89–92.

Eisinger, Chester E. "Carson McCullers and the Failure of Dialogue." *Fiction of the Forties*. Chicago: U of Chicago P, 1963. 243–58.

Eliot, T. S. "The Wasteland." 1922. *Collected Poems: 1909–1962*. London: Faber, 1963. 63–79.

Elliot, Emory, ed. *Columbia Literary History of the United States*. New York: Columbia UP, 1988.

Evans, Oliver. *Carson McCullers: Her Life and Work*. London: Owen, 1965.

———. "The Case of the Silent Singer: A Revaluation of *The Heart Is a Lonely Hunter*." *Georgia Review* 19 (1965): 188–203.

Feldman, Jessica R. *Gender on the Divide: The Dandy in Modernist Literature*. Ithaca: Cornell UP, 1993.

Fiedler, Leslie A. *An End to Innocence: Essays on Culture and Politics*. Boston: Beacon, 1966.

———. *Freaks: Myths and Images of the Secret Self*. London: Penguin, 1978.

———. *Love and Death in the American Novel*. 1960. London: Cape, 1967.

———. *No! In Thunder*. Boston: Deacon, 1960.

Fleenor, Juliann E., ed. *The Female Gothic*. Montreal: Eden, 1983.

Foucault, Michel. *The Foucault Reader*. Ed. Paul Rabinow. London: Penguin, 1991.

———. *The History of Sexuality*. Vol. 1: *An Introduction*. 1978. Trans. Robert Hurley. London: Penguin, 1990.

———. *The History of Sexuality*. Vol. 2: *The Use of Pleasure*. 1978. Trans. Robert Hurley. New York: Vintage, 1990.

Frazier, Adelaide H. "Terminal Metaphors for Love." *Pembroke Magazine* 20 (1988): 77–81.

Freud, Sigmund. "Beyond the Pleasure Principle." 1920. The Standard Edition of *The Complete Psychological Works of Sigmund Freud*. Vol. 11. Trans. James Strachey. London: Penguin, 1984. 269–338.

———. "The Economic Problem of Masochism." 1924. The Standard Edition of *The Complete Psychological Works of Sigmund Freud*. Vol. 11. Trans. James Strachey. London: Penguin, 1984. 409–26.

———. "The Ego and the Id." 1923. The Standard Edition of *The Complete Psychological Works of Sigmund Freud*. Vol. 11. Trans. James Strachey. London: Penguin, 1984. 339–407.

———. "Infantile Sexuality." 1905. The Standard Edition of *The Complete Psychological Works of Sigmund Freud*. Vol. 7. Trans. James Strachey. London: Penguin, 1984. 88–126.

———. "Medusa's Head." 1922. The Standard Edition of *The Complete Psychological Works of Sigmund Freud*. Vol. 18. Trans. James Strachey. London: Penguin, 1984. 273–74.

———. "The Sexual Aberrations." 1905. The Standard Edition of *The Complete Psychological Works of Sigmund Freud*. Vol. 7. Trans. James Strachey. London: Penguin, 1984. 45–87.

Garber, Marjorie B. *Vested Interests: Cross-Dressing and Cultural Anxiety.* New York: Routledge, 1992.

———. *Vice Versa: Bisexuality and the Eroticism of Everyday Life.* London: Hamilton, 1995.

Gatens, Moira. "A Critique of the Sex/Gender Distinction." *Beyond Marxism: Interventions after Marx.* Ed. Judith Allen and Paul Patton. Sydney: Intervention, 1983. 143–61.

Gervin, Mary A. "McCullers' Frames of Reference in *The Ballad of the Sad Café.*" *Pembroke Magazine* 20 (1988): 37–42.

Gilbert, Sandra M. "Costumes of the Mind: Transvestism as Metaphor in Modern Literature." *Critical Inquiry* 7 (1980): 391–417.

Gilbert, Sandra, and Susan Gubar. *No Man's Land: The Place of the Woman Writer in the Twentieth Century.* Vol. 2: *Sexchanges.* New Haven: Yale UP, 1989.

Ginsberg, Elaine. "The Female Initiation Theme in American Fiction." *Studies in American Fiction* 3 (1975): 27–38.

Ginsburg, Ruth. "The Pregnant Text: Bakhtin's Ur Chronotope: The Womb." *Bakhtin: Carnival and Other Subjects: Selected Papers from the 5th International Bakhtin Conference.* Amsterdam: Rodopi, 1993. 165–76.

Gossett, Louise Y. "Dispossessed Love: Carson McCullers." *Violence in Recent Southern Fiction.* Durham: Duke UP, 1965. 159–77.

Graver, Lawrence. "Carson McCullers." *Seven American Women Writers of the Twentieth Century: An Introduction.* Ed. Maureen Howard. 1963. Minneapolis: U of Minnesota P, 1977. 265–310.

Griffith, Albert J. "Carson McCullers' Myth of the Sad Cafe." *The Georgia Review* 21.1 (1967): 46–56.

Grosz, Elizabeth. "The Phallic Mother." *Feminism and Psychoanalysis: A Critical Dictionary.* Ed. Elizabeth Wright. Oxford: Blackwell, 1992. 314–15.

———. *Volatile Bodies: Toward a Corporeal Feminism.* Sydney: Allen, 1994.

Halperin, David. "Historicizing the Sexual Body: Sexual Preferences and Erotic Identities in the Pseudo-Lucianic Erôtes." *Discourses of Sexuality: From Aristotle to AIDS.* Ed. Domna C. Stanton. Ann Arbor: U of Michigan P, 1992. 236–61.

———. *One Hundred Years of Homosexuality and Other Essays on Greek Love.* New York: Routledge, 1990.

Haraway, Donna. "A Manifesto for Cyborgs: Science, Technology, and Socialist Feminism in the 1980s." *Socialist Review* 80 (1985): 65–107.

Harpham, Geoffrey Galt. *On the Grotesque: Strategies of Contradiction in Art and Literature.* Princeton: Princeton UP, 1982.

Hassan, Ihab. "Carson McCullers: The Alchemy of Love and Aesthetics of Pain." *Modern Fiction Studies* 5 (1959–60): 311–26.

———. "The Character of Post-War Fiction in America." *English Journal* 51.1 (1962): 1–8.

———. *Contemporary American Literature, 1945–1972: An Introduction*. New York: Ungar, 1973.

———. "The Idea of Adolescence in American Fiction." *American Quarterly* 10 (1958): 312–24.

———. *Radical Innocence: Studies in the Contemporary American Novel*. Princeton: Princeton UP, 1961.

Heath, Stephen. "Joan Riviere and the Masquerade." *Formations of Fantasy*. Ed. Victor Burgin, James Donald, and Cora Kaplan. London: Routledge, 1989. 45–61.

Heilbrun, Carolyn. "Androgyny and the Psychology of Sex Differences." *The Future of Difference*. Ed. Hester Eisenstein and Alice Jardine. Boston: Hall, 1980. 258–66.

———. *Toward a Recognition of Androgyny*. New York: Knopf, 1973.

Holmlund, Chris. "Masculinity as Multiple Masquerade: The 'Mature' Stallone and the Stallone Clone." *Screening the Male: Exploring Masculinities in Hollywood Cinema*. Ed. Steven Cohan and Ina Rae Hark. London: Routledge, 1993. 213–29.

Howard, Maureen. "Introduction." *Seven American Women Writers of the Twentieth Century: An Introduction*. 1963. Minneapolis: U of Minnesota P, 1977. 3–27.

Huf, Linda. "*The Heart Is a Lonely Hunter*: Carson McCuller's [*sic*] Young Woman with a Great Future behind Her." *A Portrait of the Artist as a Young Woman: The Writer as Heroine in American Literature*. New York: Ungar, 1983. 105–23.

Irigaray, Luce. *Speculum of the Other Woman*. Trans. Gillian C. Gill. Ithaca: Cornell UP, 1985.

———. *This Sex Which Is Not One*. Trans. Catherine Porter with Carolyn Burke. Ithaca: Cornell UP, 1985.

James, Judith Giblin. *Wunderkind: The Reputation of Carson McCullers, 1940–1990*. Columbia, SC: Camden, 1995.

Johnson, James William. "The Adolescent Hero: A Trend in Modern Fiction." *Twentieth Century Literature* 5.1 (1959): 3–11.

Johstoneaux, Raphael. "The Forces of Dehumanization: *Reflections in a Golden Eye*." *Encyclia* 66 (1989): 97–104.

Jong, Erica. *Fear of Flying: A Novel*. New York: Holt, 1973.

Kahane, Claire. "The Gothic Mirror." *The (M)other Tongue: Essays in Feminist*

Psychoanalytic Interpretation. Ed. Shirley Nelson Garner, Claire Kahane, and Madelon Sprengnether. Ithaca: Cornell UP, 1985. 334–51.

———. "The Maternal Legacy: The Grotesque Tradition in Flannery O'Connor's Female Gothic." *The Female Gothic*. Ed. Juliann E. Fleenor. Montreal: Eden, 1983. 242–56.

Kenschaft, Lori. "Homoerotics and Human Connections: Reading Carson McCullers 'As a Lesbian.'" *Critical Essays on Carson McCullers*. Ed. Beverley Lyon Clark and Melvyn J. Friedman. New York: Hall, 1996. 220–33.

Kestler, Frances. "Gothic Influence of the Grotesque Characters of the Lonely Hunter." *Pembroke Magazine* 20 (1988): 30–36.

Kissel, Susan. "Carson McCullers's 'Wunderkind': A Case Study in Female Adolescence." *Kentucky Philological Review* 6 (1991): 15–20.

Korenman, Joan S. "Carson McCullers' 'Proletarian Novel.'" *Studies in the Humanities* 5 (1976): 8–13.

Lacan, Jacques. "The Signification of the Phallus." *Écrits: A Selection*. Trans. Alan Sheridan. New York: Norton, 1977. 281–91.

Lawrence, D. H. "The Prussian Officer." 1914. *The Prussian Officer and Other Stories*. London: Penguin, 1945. 7–29.

Madden, David. "The Paradox of the Need for Privacy and the Need for Understanding in Carson McCullers' *The Heart Is a Lonely Hunter*." *Literature and Psychology* 17.2–3 (1967): 128–40.

Malin, Irving. *New American Gothic*. Carbondale: Southern Illinois UP, 1962.

McBride, Mary. "Loneliness and Longing in Selected Plays of Carson McCullers and Tennessee Williams." *Modern American Drama: The Female Canon*. Ed. June Schlueter. Rutherford, NJ: Fairleigh Dickinson UP, 1990. 143–50.

McDowell, Margaret B. *Carson McCullers*. Boston: Twayne, 1980.

McHale, Brian. *Postmodernist Fiction*. London: Routledge, 1989.

Melville, Herman. *Billy Budd, Sailor and Other Stories*. 1962. London: Penguin, 1967.

Miles, Rosalind. *The Fiction of Sex: Themes and Functions of Sex Difference in the Modern Novel*. London: Vision, 1974.

Millichap, Joseph R. "Carson McCullers' Literary Ballad." *Georgia Review* 27 (1973): 329–39.

———. "Distorted Matter and Disjunctive Forms: The Grotesque as Modernist Genre." *Arizona Quarterly* 33 (1977): 339–47.

———. "The Realistic Structure of *The Heart Is a Lonely Hunter*." *Twentieth Century Literature* 17.1 (1971): 11–17.

Moers, Ellen. *Literary Women*. London: Allen, 1977.

Moi, Toril. *Sexual/Textual Politics: Feminist Literary Theory*. London: Routledge, 1988.

Morson, Gary Saul, and Caryl Emerson. *Mikhail Bakhtin: Creation of a Prosaics*. Stanford: Stanford UP, 1990.

Nagpal, Pratibha. "The Element of Grotesque in *Reflections in a Golden Eye* and *The Ballad of the Sad Café* by Carson McCullers." *Punjab University Research Bulletin (Arts)* 18.2 (1987): 61–66.

O'Connor, Flannery. *Mystery and Manners: Occasional Prose*. 1969. Ed. Sally and Robert Fitzgerald. New York: Noonday, 1994.

———. "A Temple of the Holy Ghost." *A Good Man Is Hard to Find*. 1948. London: Women's Press, 1980. 85–101.

———. *Wise Blood*. 1949. New York: Noonday, 1995.

Ovid. *Metamorphoses*. Trans. Rolfe Humphries. Bloomington: Indiana UP, 1955.

Pacteau, Francette. "The Impossible Referent: Representations of the Androgyne." *Formations of Fantasy*. Ed. Victor Burgin, James Donald, and Cora Kaplan. London: Routledge, 1989. 62–84.

Paden, Frances Freeman. "Autistic Gestures in *The Heart Is a Lonely Hunter*." *Modern Fiction Studies* 28 (1982): 453–63.

Paulson, Suzanne Morrow. "Carson McCullers's *The Ballad of the Sad Café*: A Song Half Sung, Misogyny, and 'Ganging Up.'" *Critical Essays on Carson McCullers*. Ed. Beverley Lyon Clark and Melvyn J. Friedman. New York: Hall, 1996. 187–205.

Perry, Constance M. "Carson McCullers and the Female *Wunderkind*." *Southern Literary Journal* 19 (1986): 36–45.

Peterson, Shirley. "Freaking Feminism: *The Life and Loves of a She-Devil* and *Nights at the Circus* as Narrative Freak Show." *Freakery: Cultural Spectacles of the Extraordinary Body*. Ed. Rosemarie Garland Thomson. New York: New York UP, 1996. 291–301.

Petry, Alice Hall. "Carson McCullers's Precocious 'Wunderkind.'" *Southern Quarterly* 26.3 (1988): 31–39.

Phillips, Robert S. "Dinesen's 'Monkey' and McCullers' 'Ballad': A Study in Literary Affinity." *Studies in Short Fiction* 1 (1964): 184–90.

———. "The Gothic Architecture of *The Member of the Wedding*." *Renascence* 16 (1964): 59–72.

Plato. *Symposium*. Trans. Walter Hamilton. Middlesex: Penguin, 1951.

Rechnitz, Robert M. "The Failure of Love: The Grotesque in Two Novels by Carson McCullers." *Georgia Review* 22.4 (1968): 454–63.

Rich, Nancy B. "The 'Ironic Parable of Fascism' in *The Heart Is a Lonely Hunter*." *Southern Literary Journal* 9 (1977): 108–23.

Richards, Gary. "Another Southern Renaissance: Sexual Otherness in Mid-Twentieth Century Southern Fiction." Diss. Vanderbilt U, 1996.

Riviere, Joan. "Womanliness as a Masquerade." 1929. *Formations of Fantasy*. Ed. Victor Burgin, James Donald, and Cora Kaplan. London: Routledge, 1989. 35–44.

Roberts, Mary. "Imperfect Androgyny and Imperfect Love in the Works of Carson McCullers." *Studies in Literature* 12.2 (1980): 73–98.

Robinson, Sally. *Engendering the Subject: Gender and Self-Representation in Contemporary Women's Fiction*. Albany: State U of New York P, 1991.

Roth, Marty. "Homosexual Expression and Homophobic Censorship: The Situation of the Text." *Camp Grounds: Style and Homosexuality*. Ed. David Bergman. Amherst: U of Massachusetts P, 1993. 268–81.

Ruland, Richard, and Malcolm Bradbury. *From Puritanism to Postmodernism: A History of American Literature*. New York: Penguin, 1991.

Russo, Mary. *The Female Grotesque: Risk, Excess and Modernity*. New York: Routledge, 1994.

Sarotte, Georges-Michel. *Like a Brother, Like a Lover: Male Homosexuality in the American Novel and Theater from Herman Melville to James Baldwin*. Trans. Richard Miller. Garden City, NY: Anchor, 1978.

Schor, Naomi. "This Essentialism Which Is Not One: Coming to Grips with Irigaray." *Difference* 1.2 (1989): 38–58.

———. "Dreaming Dissymmetry: Barthes, Foucault, and Sexual Difference." *Men in Feminism*. Ed. Alice Jardine and Paul Smith. New York: Methuen, 1987. 98–110.

Schorer, Mark. "Carson McCullers and Truman Capote." *The World We Imagine: Selected Essays*. London: Chatto, 1969. 274–96.

Secor, Cynthia, ed. *The Androgyny Papers*. Special edition of *Women's Studies* 2 (1974).

Sedgwick, Eve Kosofsky. *Between Men: English Literature and Male Homosocial Desire*. New York: Columbia UP, 1985.

———. *Epistemology of the Closet*. Berkeley: U of California P, 1990.

Segrest, Mab. *My Mama's Dead Squirrel: Lesbian Essays on Southern Culture*. Ithaca, NY: Firebrand, 1985.

Showalter, Elaine. *The Female Malady: Women, Madness and English Culture, 1830–1980*. London: Virago, 1987.

———. *A Literature of Their Own: British Women Novelists from Brontë to Lessing*. London: Virago, 1978.

Silverman, Kaja. *Male Subjectivity at the Margins*. New York: Routledge, 1992.

Sinfield, Alan. *The Wilde Century: Effeminacy, Oscar Wilde and the Queer Moment*. New York: Columbia UP, 1994.

Singer, June. *Androgyny: Towards a New Theory of Sexuality*. New York: Anchor, 1976.

Snider, Clifton. "Jungian Theory, Its Literary Application, and a Discussion of *The Member of the Wedding*." *Psychological Perspectives on Literature: Freudian Dissidents and Non-Freudians: A Casebook*. Ed. Joseph Natoli. Hamden, CT: Archon, 1984. 13–42.

Sosnoski, Karen. "Society's Freaks: The Effects of Sexual Stereotyping in Carson McCullers' Fiction." *Pembroke Magazine* 20 (1988): 82–88.

Spelman, Elizabeth. "Woman as Body: Ancient and Contemporary Views." *Feminist Studies* 8.1 (1982): 109–31.

Spiegel, Alan. "A Theory of the Grotesque in Southern Fiction." *Georgia Review* 26 (1972): 426–37.

Spivak, Gayatri Chakravorty. "Displacement and the Discourse of Woman." *Displacement: Derrida and After*. Ed. Mark Krupnick. Bloomington: Indiana UP, 1983. 169–95.

———. "Three Feminist Readings: McCullers, Drabble, Habermas." *Union Seminary Quarterly Review* 35.1–2 (1979–80): 15–34.

Stafford, Tony. "'Gray Eyes Is Glass': Image and Theme in *The Member of the Wedding*." *American Drama* 3 (1993): 54–66.

Stallybrass, Peter, and Allon White. *The Politics and Poetics of Transgression*. Ithaca: Cornell UP, 1986.

Stewart, Susan. *On Longing: Narratives of the Miniature, the Gigantic, the Souvenir, the Collection*. Durham: Duke UP, 1993.

Taetzsch, L. "Crossing Trajectories in *The Heart Is a Lonely Hunter*." *New Orleans Review* 19 (1992): 192–97.

Thomas, Leroy. "Carson McCullers: The Plight of the Lonely Hunter." *Pembroke Magazine* 20 (1988): 10–15.

Thomson, Rosemarie Garland. *Extraordinary Bodies: Figuring Physical Disability in American Culture and Literature*. New York: Columbia UP, 1997.

———, ed. *Freakery: Cultural Spectacles of the Extraordinary Body*. New York: New York UP, 1996.

Vande Kieft, Ruth M. "The Love Ethos of Porter, Welty, and McCullers." *The Female Tradition in Southern Literature*. Ed. Carol S. Manning. Urbana: U of Illinois P, 1993. 235–58.

Van O'Connor, William. *The Grotesque: An American Genre and Other Essays*. Carbondale: Southern Illinois UP, 1962.

Walsh, Margaret. "Carson McCullers' Anti-Fairy Tale: *The Ballad of the Sad Café*." *Pembroke Magazine* 20 (1988): 43–48.
Warner, Marina. *Joan of Arc: The Image of Female Heroism*. New York: Knopf, 1981.
Weeks, Jeffrey. *Sex, Politics and Society: The Regulation of Sexuality since 1800*. London: Longman, 1981.
——. *Sexuality and Its Discontents: Meanings, Myths and Modern Sexualities*. London: Routledge, 1985.
Weil, Kari. *Androgyny and the Denial of Difference*. Charlottesville: UP of Virginia, 1992.
Weinstock, Jeffrey A. "Freaks in Space: 'Extraterrestrialism' and 'Deep Space Multiculturalism.'" *Freakery: Cultural Spectacles of the Extraordinary Body*. Ed. Rosemarie Garland Thomson. New York: New York UP, 1996. 327–37.
Westling, Louise. *Sacred Groves and Ravaged Gardens: The Fiction of Eudora Welty, Carson McCullers, and Flannery O'Connor*. Athens: U of Georgia P, 1985.
White, Barbara. "Loss of Self in Carson McCullers' *The Member of the Wedding*." *Growing Up Female: Adolescent Girlhood in American Fiction*. Westport, CT: Greenwood, 1985. 89–111.
Whitt, Jan. "The Loneliest Hunter." *Southern Literary Journal* 24 (1992): 26–35.
Whitt, Mary A. "The Mutes in Carson McCullers' *The Heart Is a Lonely Hunter*." *Pembroke Magazine* 20 (1988): 24–29.
Woolf, Virginia. *The Essays of Virginia Woolf: Volume 2, 1912–1918*. Ed. Andrew McNeillie. London: Hogarth, 1987.
——. *A Room of One's Own*. *A Room of One's Own and Three Guineas*. 1929. London: Hogarth, 1984.
Yaeger, Patricia. "Beyond the Hummingbird: Southern Women Writers and the Southern Gargantua." *Haunted Bodies: Gender and Southern Texts*. Ed. Anne Goodwyn Jones and Susan V. Donaldson. Charlottesville: UP of Virginia, 1997. 287–318.
——. *Dirt and Desire: Reconstructing Southern Women's Writing, 1930–1990*. Chicago: U of Chicago P, 2000.
——. "Edible Labor." *Southern Quarterly* 30.2–3 (1992): 150–59.

Index